PRINCIPLES

of

MEDITATION

PRINCIPLES
of
MEDITATION

Eastern Wisdom for the Western Mind

C. Alexander Simpkins, Ph.D.
&
Annellen M. Simpkins, Ph.D.

TUTTLE PUBLISHING
BOSTON ❧ RUTLAND, VERMONT ❧ TOKYO

First published in 1996 by Tuttle Publishing, an imprint of Periplus Editions (HK) Ltd., with editorial offices at 153 Milk Street, Boston, Massachusetts, 02109.

Library of Congress Cataloging-in-Publication Data

Simpkins, C. Alexander.
    Principles of meditation : Eastern wisdom for the Western mind / Charles Alexander Simpkins & Annellen M. Simpkins. — 1st ed.
        p. cm.
    Includes bibliographical references (p.).
    ISBN 0-8048-3074-6
    1. Meditation. I. Simpkins, Annellen M. II. Title.
BL627.S55 1996
291.4'3—dc20   96-437
                                                               CIP

Distributed by

USA	JAPAN
Tuttle Publishing	Tuttle Shokai Ltd
Distribution Center	1-21-13, Seki
Airport Industrial Park	Tama-ku, Kawasaki-shi
364 Innovation Drive	Kanagawa-ken 214-0022, Japan
North Clarendon, VT 05759-9436	Tel: (044) 833-0225
Tel: (802) 773-8930	Fax: (044) 822-0413
Tel: (800) 526-2778	

CANADA	SOUTHEAST ASIA
Raincoast Books	Berkeley Books Pte Ltd
8680 Cambie Street	5 Little Road #08-01
Vancouver, British Columbia	Singapore 536983
V6P 6M9	Tel: (65) 280-1330
Tel: (604) 323-7100	Fax: (65) 280-6290
Fax: (604) 323-2600	

Book design by Jill Winitzer
Cover art by Carmen Z. Simpkins

Carmen Z. Simpkins' abstract expressionist paintings suggest mood, movement, and mysticism. Simpkins has been painting for 74 years. Her first solo show took place in Camden, Maine, in 1962 at the Broadlawn Gallery. She has exhibited throughout the world and her works are in private collections in Europe and North America. She continues to paint at her studio-gallery in Sebastian, Florida.

First edition
05 04 03 02 01 00 99   10 9 8 7 6 5 4

Printed in the United States of America

CONTENTS

We dedicate this book to our parents,
Carmen and Nat Simpkins and
Naomi and Herbert Minkin.

INTRODUCTION
WHAT IS MEDITATION?

Nothing is impossible to a willing mind.
—Book of the Han Dynasty cited in
Zen in the Martial Arts by Joe Hyams

P eople who do not know much about meditation often think of it in a limited sense, as deep thought or contemplation. Even *Webster's Dictionary* defines meditation narrowly: "To reflect on; ponder. To engage in contemplation." From its long and rich early history, to its widespread and diverse practice today, meditation includes thinking, but it is a much broader and fuller endeavor. No standard definition includes all types of meditation. Attempting to confine it to a simple definition is like trying to summarize a play by Shakespeare in only one sentence.

Meditation brings about the union of opposites, a balance between many factors. The ancient yin-yang symbol depicts this union of opposites. Within the white there is black, and within the black there is white. The two sides intertwine, one with the other. When we explore the mind, the body is affected. When we work with the conscious mind, the unconscious mind becomes involved. Sometimes we empty the mind of all thoughts; sometimes we fill it by focusing on a specific thought. As skill develops in meditation, there is a balance: union.

What is clear is that first and foremost, meditation is an experience. The experience is so highly valued that it is considered an inward "art." Though the meditator returns to the center within the self, paradoxically he or she may transcend the limitations imposed on the self.

The essence of meditation is an experience. We encourage you to make it a personal experience, not just an abstract one. You can extend your mind more than you would imagine. The link is there intuitively. This use of your mind will connect you to the source of thinking: a deeper, more profound state.

You can learn to meditate without elaborate technological equipment, esoteric training, or vast expense. Yet its effects are deep, long-lasting, and profound. You can lose little by experimenting with it as an experience, and gain much. Meditation has no unpleasant side effects, as with drugs or some other treatments. As time passes and your experience grows, meditation will take on a personal aspect, which changes its meaning for you. And through meditation, you will grow better and wiser, fulfilling yourself in life with more satisfaction and calmer reactions.

Meditation practices are used in every country, all over the world. Each of the major Eastern religions has its own approach. There are many paths to choose from, and our intent is not to proselytize anyone but rather to look for the common factors of Eastern meditation and draw out methods that can be applied to everyday life. These methods are latent with positive potential. The personal experiences you bring to these meditation exercises will make them your own.

TYPES OF MEDITATION

To the beginner, the world of meditation can be bewildering. Over thousands of years, a myriad of meditation methods have developed.

INTRODUCTION

We have studied and extracted for you some of the common themes that run throughout the many traditions. Later in the book, you will have the opportunity to experiment personally with all of these types of meditation practices, thereby touching upon many of the great meditation traditions of the world.

Meditation methods may be classified in terms of the yin-yang concept. Thus, meditation may be active (yang) or passive (yin). This means that meditators either use their will and effort to do something with their mind, or they wait passively and allow things to happen. Today, we are all accustomed to being busy and active. Therefore, the active forms of meditation may make more sense at first. But passive, not-doing, waiting, letting-be, or allowing is a valuable complement that may open up an entirely new realm of possibilities. An attitude of passive waiting and allowing often makes it easier to call forth the unconscious. You will find both passive and active meditation exercises in Parts Two and Three.

Some forms of meditation aim to empty the mind of all thoughts, while others try to fill it with chosen thoughts. Taoist practitioners believe that through the calm, empty mind, the spirit of the Tao, that is, the creative principle that orders the universe, is then able to enter. Certain Yoga and Buddhist meditation sects believe that filling the entire mind with a wonderful, pure thought will raise practitioners to a more enlightened plane.

Other meditation styles teach meditators to withdraw from the external world. The rationales may vary: some believe the world of humankind and its activities are superficial or even unreal. Therefore, to withdraw from the world of events is a step toward a more fundamental and real reality. Taking this position to the extreme, people may withdraw into monasteries or live as hermits alone on mountains or in caves, for a life that is pure and devoid of worldly concerns.

An opposite belief is that we live our lives alienated from ourselves and that fully immersing ourselves in our being will lead to an integrated wholeness, a revelation. The meditation style of Zen Buddhism teaches practitioners to give up the concept of a split between thought and action, to unify and thereby live fully in the moment, so that even mundane tasks can be used for profound meditation.

Meditation sometimes specifies what meditators should attend to. For some, the object of meditation is to be directed to the inner realm. Thus, you close your eyes and imagine or think about something within your mind. Other styles focus on the outer, such as "Think of a tree. Meditate on all aspects of it."

These qualities of meditation fall under the yin-yang, the union of opposites, in which all become one in the Tao, bringing about a higher consciousness.

HOW TO USE THIS BOOK

The past is rich with ancient wisdom upon which modern meditators can draw. Part One acquaints you with several of the most profound theories of meditation from history. In Part Two we teach you the skills needed to begin your own meditation. Part Three guides you through actual meditation practices that draw upon the skills learned in the previous section. Finally, Part Four offers specific applications for meditation in a number of areas, which you can use as springboards for other areas.

We have worked out a method of meditation that is highly effective and useful. As your abilities evolve, you will find that meditation is easier for you. It becomes a natural expression of your individuality, leading to better use of your potential. The potential is the "not yet" waiting in the wings, so to speak. The "actual" is what takes place on the stage. Many people fail to differentiate these two areas, yet they are separate. Meditation will teach you to draw from your potential to enhance the actual, to increase the range of what you can do.

Throughout the book we provide exercises that give you an opportunity to experiment with the concepts as they are introduced, to make them your own. Note that "experiment" should be understood in its classic sense, of trying the exercise without any preconceived idea of what you will experience. Allow your reactions without interfering, and make note of them mentally. Experiment, observe, and explore with a curious, open attitude. Some people may want to keep a written journal of their experiences, but this is not required.

In order to experiment, it helps to take on a nonjudgmental attitude. What this means is that you should not try to decide whether your experience is good or bad. As the nineteenth-century phenomenological philosopher Edmund Husserl said, "Put it in brackets." Simply notice your reactions and experiences and put them aside. Suspend your judgment or belief temporarily. If you do this, you will find that your mind is freer and more able to respond to the exercises. Meditate as often as you can. Some people will set aside a regular time of the day for meditating. For others, meditating may be less structured. Learn to work with your own natural tendencies, but whatever you do, be sure to meditate as much as possible. Give the meditation exercises some time to affect you, or perhaps for the effects to become noticeable.

Read each exercise over several times. Then put the book aside and try it. Do not worry if you forget some of the instructions. You will use what is most important to you. Feel free to go through the exercises many times. Creative variations may occur to you as you learn how to use these concepts. You may be surprised to make new discoveries later, and we hope you will have fun in the process

PART ONE

Great Traditions
of Meditation

This human mind wrote history, and this must read it.
—Ralph Waldo Emerson, "History"

History is usually traced through events, dates, rulers, and wars. Yet if you carefully inspect the tapestry of history, a hidden thread runs through it all, creating the patterns. Beneath, like an underground spring, is the river of the mind, always flowing, always reaching onward, seeking to unravel the mysteries of life and fulfill its destiny. Meditation has been practiced for centuries and has been a primary tool in the discovery of meaning itself. The ancient methods still followed today are patterned on the wisdom of the ancestors. If we look back through the ages, we find several great styles of meditation, all of which endure today. In the following pages we explain a number of the significant forms to serve as background for our meditation approach. After you learn about these various meditative approaches, you will be ready to develop personal skills that will help you find a source of inner strength through meditation. How you use this inner strength is up to you.

The great traditions of meditation we discuss will put you in touch with the deeper pools of insight from the past. Then, through guidance and exercises, we will show you how to make the best insights of these theories a useful addition to your own meditative abilities.

1
YOGA: MASTER YOUR MIND

It is good to know that the ancient thinkers required of us to realize the possibilities of the soul in solitude and silence, and to transform the flashing and fading moments of vision into a steady light which could illumine the long years of life.

—Radhakrishnan

India has long been a country steeped in a spiritual quest for higher consciousness. As Lin Yutang, a scholar of Eastern philosophy, once said, "India is a land and a people intoxicated with God." Yoga is one of the Indian philosophies of higher consciousness. It uses meditation purposefully to reach beyond everyday life.

BLESSED LORD'S SONG

Yoga was dramatized as part of a famous epic known as the *Bhagavad-Gita*, the Blessed Lord's Song. This ancient epic describes Yoga as a solution offered by divine inspiration to the protagonist's problems of life. Arjuna, a great warrior, was about to face a mighty battle between good and evil. Just before the beginning of the fight, he realized that he cared about kinsmen and others on both sides. Arjuna refused both to fight and to kill. He laid down his weapons, overcome with sadness,

In a long and detailed dialogue, the god Krishna, disguised as Arjuna's charioteer, explains the applications of each type of Yoga to help Arjuna face his duty and defend his country.

Krishna advises Arjuna to be himself, to act according to his own true nature. "If you are in the world of work, work fully without anger or cravings." Arjuna came from the warrior class, so fighting was his appropriate role of action. Krishna explained that it was his duty to be at one with his nature, to express his nature, but in terms of its highest expression. Warriors should be brave, skilled, and firm. Arjuna should perform his actions without attachment to the fruits of his actions. When Arjuna asked whether his kinsmen would die if he followed through with the war, Krishna answered that no one would be killed, really, because men's souls are immortal. An unmanifested world beyond always exists and is never destroyed. If Arjuna devoted himself to Krishna, who is everything and oneness, he would have nothing to fear. The legend ends with Arjuna's resolve to follow his destiny wholeheartedly.

In modern times, we have come to value peace and ideally fight in battle only when a great threat to freedom or ideals arises, but Krishna's words can be applied to all actions: all actions should be in keeping with your true nature and done completely. Yoga's wisdom transcends its context. Yoga practice gives you the ability to discipline and control your mind so that you can carry out your life's work.

YOGA ROOTS

Yoga, in ancient Sanskrit, means "union" or "to yoke." The word wended its way through Anglo-Saxon English as "yueg" to become the modern word *yoke*. Yoga is a method of personal discipline by which "to harness the body to the soul and the soul to the universal soul," according to *Webster's Dictionary*. The Yogi seeks *samadhi*, enlightenment, by withdrawing the mind from involvement with externals to focus on higher consciousness. By practicing Yoga you can bring this about.

Yoga holds that there is an unchanging essence within us, a self, a soul called Atman. This individual soul is a microcosm in which is reflected the macrocosm of the universe. It is a little drop of the ocean of Universal Soul or Universal Consciousness, where mind, energy, and matter are linked in one manifestation. Energy is intelligent and mind is its origin. Through meditative practice, people can learn to control and direct their minds so that this higher consciousness of the universe is realized and experienced. The experience of this higher consciousness is referred to as *nirvana*. It results in enjoyable, positive experiences of unity, oneness with the universe, at will.

Breathing and breath control play a primary role in opening the doorway to the mind. Using breath the Yogi takes control of the body and mind, to send vital energy, called *prana*, where it is needed for health and strength, to steady the emotions and bring inner development. Breathing rhythmically, timed to the pulse rate, links breathing to the metabolic state and to the emotions. Through this link, practitioners gain access to involuntary processes such as pulse rate and body temperature. Certain meditative postures enhance the practice of rhythmic breathing, and the exact science of using these techniques is taught in Hatha Yoga.

Prana is to Hindu philosophy what chi is to the Chinese, an all-pervading principle of life force and energy. Prana is the air, yet not of the air: it is in all matter. Without prana, we are like a circuit with no electricity. By using concentration and visualization, we can absorb and store prana within the center of the psychic body. Then it can be used or even externalized both to heal and to recharge the batteries of life.

YOGA BRANCHES

There are many branches or systems of Yoga, each of which has a specific emphasis or path of practices to follow as a route to enlightenment. Hatha Yoga uses a group of body postures to focus and control the mind. Pranayama, which is part of Hatha Yoga, employs rhythmic structured and tuned breathing exercises to gain control of the involuntary muscles, cure illness, affect energy, and still the mind. From all of the different branches of Yoga, higher states of consciousness may be achieved that make possible great feats of control of involuntary functions; some skilled Yogis can actually alter their heart rates at will.

Patanjali, who codified Yoga, describes eight "limbs" or stages by which people can reach enlightenment. The proper practice of Yoga includes a strict code of ethical conduct for those who travel along this path. These eight limbs begin with level one, the Yamas, ten prohibitions or acts that Yogis must never commit, such as killing, stealing, or lying. The next level, Niyama, guides Yogis in what they should do: be modest, live simply, be tolerant, sincere, practice both mental and physical hygiene, and so on. At level three, the practitioner learns Asanas, postures and exercises done in Hatha Yoga. Breath control is mastered at the fourth level, called Pranayama. Pratyahara or withdrawal of the senses is practiced at level five. Yogis develop concentration, Dharana, at the sixth level. The seventh level is devoted to meditation, Dhyana. This leads to the highest level, *samadhi*, spiritual enlightenment.

Each of the Yoga systems takes a somewhat different position with respect to what the aspirant's lifestyle orientation must be, but it is perfectly feasible to combine elements of several systems to individualize a program. Yoga can be practiced by people of all walks of life because it offers so many options. While starting from differing emphases, depending on the system, all forms of Yoga lead to the same goal. For instance, an academically inclined, philosophical individual might turn to Gnani Yoga, which emphasizes wisdom, while a health-care practitioner might prefer Bhakti Yoga, which stresses love. Businesspeople and merchants will find relevant learnings from Karma Yoga, where the emphasis is on work. The many other forms of Yoga offer infinite possible intercombinations. Each of these Yoga systems trains practitioners to transcend their individual selves. A number of the types of Yoga important to meditation are described in the following sections.

Hatha Yoga

Placing the body in a straight posture, with the chest, throat, and head held erect, making the organs together with the mind, perfectly established in the lotus of the heart, the sage crosses all the fearful currents of ignorance by means of the raft of Brahman.

—The Upanishads

Hatha Yoga is the form of Yoga that is familiar to most people. The Hatha Yoga system uses a series of from 84 to 840,000 postures, called asanas, in which rhythmic patterns of breath control and concentration are applied to strengthen, tone, and activate the body and its corresponding energy centers, known as *chakras*. Thus yogis can purify their bodies and withdraw their minds from distractions from the outside world to be free to achieve higher consciousness. Union with the unconscious in samadhi, or enlightenment, becomes possible. The result of Hatha Yoga practice is health, cleanliness, good diet, and long life. In Hatha Yoga the path to the mind is through the body. This system is often combined with other systems of Yoga for complete development.

Raja Yoga

In Raja Yoga, or Royal Yoga, physical postures are considered of less importance. Higher consciousness is attained through direct training and control of the mind. Greater, more accurate focused attention, perception, and intense concentration help to clear the field of the mind for enlightenment. Raja Yoga also has techniques for stilling the mind and uses the eight limbs of Yoga to permit the true self to shine through. For it is believed that the source of enlightenment and deeper wisdom is within oneself.

Raja Yoga teaches and disciplines the practitioner to be attuned to the Real Self within. The consciousness of the "I" is a realization that comes in time, a sense of oneself as an entity with life beyond that of the physical body, that continues beyond the body's destruction. The practice of Raja Yoga meditation leads the practitioner from the physical plane to the mental plane, of mind and thought, thence to the spiritual plane, of oneness with virtue and transcendence.

This parallels the fundamental belief of Mahayana Buddhism (described in chapter 2) that all life is the manifestation of "One Life." But Raja Yogis differ from the Buddhists in their belief that individual consciousness has reality or will. The "I" or ego is beyond the mind and, indeed, is one with all mind. In Buddhism, the ego or self is believed to be an illusion. In Yoga, everyone has a self. The self is the individual manifestation of a higher self, the Universal Oneness. Identifying with the higher self results in a feeling of expanding consciousness and oneness with the universe.

Gnani Yoga

Gnani Yoga is the Yoga of wisdom, the way of higher knowledge. It is a philosophical system of meditation by which individuals change their belief system. The personal self is given up as illusion, which permits the Universal Self, the Oneness of Being of the universe, to emerge. Gnani Yoga involves philosophical study and disciplined concentration on certain insights, so that practitioners experience their true personal identity as the Being of the universe. Gnani Yogis customarily disidentify with the body and with the individual ego or personality and contemplate themselves in terms of the larger, more complete identity. Themes of Gnani Yoga are similar to those of Buddhism. In both systems, the personal self is an illusion. Once this is accepted and experienced, a blissful feeling of oneness with "Allness" becomes manifest.

Bhakti Yoga

Bhakti Yoga is an almost Christian, saintly surrender, for those with potential for a deeply religious, self-sacrificing orientation. Love of God, to the Bhakti Yogi, is not prostration before a mighty ruler but rather a warm communion with a loving presence and a happy, joyful, natural life. The Bhakti might laugh, sing, be hopeful and optimistic, positive, and cheerful. Bhakti Yogis seek to be loving and helpful to others, which inspires all to higher values and ethics. Where Raja Yoga seeks union with the Divine within, Bhakti Yogis would deny the validity of this. Bhakti Yoga holds that God is always beyond you. Devotion to classical ideals of self sacrifice and love, selfless altruism, compassion, and kindness are the paths to follow to find enlightenment. Jesus, Buddha, Muhammad, and Mother Teresa all are, to this way of thinking, Bhakti Yogis. By the devotion of self to others, the personal ego and selfish desires can be transcended, and thereby, union with the higher self becomes possible.

Karma Yoga

Karma Yoga is an ancient Yoga of great significance to modern life, with our work ethic in our highly industrialized society. All human beings must work. Activity, action is proper. Meditation need not demand passivity.

The word *karma* comes from the root *Kr,* which means "to effect." Karma is a Yoga of cause and effect. Newton's law, that every force evokes an equal but opposite counterforce, makes an analogy with action possible: every action has an equal but opposite reaction. Our acts affect the world. Karma Yogis seek to make the effect positive.

Karma Yoga teaches about virtue, in giving charity to those in need, in preserving life whenever possible. Practitioners are encouraged to stop doing unimportant things and instead put their energies into doing good. It is better for people to be detached from the fruits of their actions and instead focus on the appropriate duties they are called to perform. Suffering may be part of the path of work, just as joy is, at times. Karma Yoga holds that people must not balk at suffering or try to avoid it, but rather enter into it wholeheartedly. The outcome is unimportant. According to Karma Yoga, work is a fitting setting within which to concentrate meditative efforts and thus achieve nirvana.

Mantra Yoga

Mantra Yoga uses verbal chants and simple sounds called mantras to concentrate and focus the energies. Words such as *Om,* which symbolizes oneness in Sanskrit, are commonly used. Tibetan Yoga extends this into more complex formulas. Entire systems of meditation can be based in Mantra Yoga. Transcendental meditation (TM) is one well-known form. After consultation and diagnosis, the guru gives an individual mantra to the practitioner. The practitioner silently repeats this mantra every day and concentrates on it for years and years, leading to enlightenment.

These pure systems illustrate some of the different emphases of the many Yoga systems. Each of these paths can lead to the goal of enlightenment, if it is followed in a disciplined, wholehearted fashion. By choosing a route appropriate to one's personality and lifestyle, anyone can follow the path.

Over the years, aspects from the pure systems have been combined in various ways: mantras of affirmation may be chanted as part of meditation in Raja Yoga, for example. Hatha Yoga practices might be used with deep concentration exercises for the mind drawn from Raja.

Yogis are sincere individuals committed to a lifelong quest. Buddhism continued many of the practices, traditions, and attitudes of Yoga but took a new perspective and point of view. Variations and versions of Yoga exist in many philosophical and practical systems today.

As a highly developed mental discipline, Yoga was the beginning. Variations and aspects of Yoga practices are included as a small part of modern philosophies of meditation, but modern methods can go beyond Yoga's parameters.

Amida Buddha
Japanese, Early Edo period (1615–1868) wood sculpture.
Bequest of Mrs. Cora Timken Burnett. San Diego Museum of Art.

2
BUDDHISM: RELEASE
FROM ILLUSION

Be a lamp unto yourself.

—Buddhist proverb

n Buddhism, the source of light is the human mind. One of the world's great religions, Buddhism, much like Yoga, has evolved over the centuries, dividing into various sects, each with its own perspectives, emphases, and practices. Despite the vast diversity in forms of Buddhism today, each group traces its roots back to one man, the founder, Siddhartha Gautama. His enlightenment experience lit the way to a new faith for more than 300 million followers around the globe.

Siddhartha was born in India, around the sixth century B.C., to a wealthy aristocratic family. His father helped rule in the district of northern India called Kapilavastu, from which the snowcapped peaks of the Himalayas could be viewed. Though his mother died only seven days after his birth, Siddhartha was raised with love. He grew into a handsome, intelligent young man, destined to follow in his father's footsteps. Siddhartha married early to one of the most beautiful women in the kingdom and had a son with her. His life seemed idyllic. He enjoyed a comfortable, sheltered family life within the luxury of the palace walls, studying Indian Yogic philosophy and meditation, with his every need met. He looked forward to caring for his subjects. Yet he carried within him a deep restlessness.

Legend has it that one day he traveled outside the palace walls to inspect his father's lands with his faithful servant Channah. By accident he chanced upon a sickly man, wracked with fever, wasting away from starvation. Siddhartha asked, "Why does he suffer so?"

His servant answered, "This is the way of life, sire. Many suffer with illness."

Later they came upon an old man, weak and dying.

Siddhartha asked again, "Why does he suffer so?"

And his servant responded tenderly, "Sire, old age and death are the way of all life. We all must die."

Siddhartha returned home deeply troubled. Feeling called upon to solve these universal problems of suffering and death, he vowed to leave the comfort of his life in the palace to find the answers for his people. He joined the forest ascetics who believed that the path to truth and wisdom was through self-denial. Siddhartha starved and disciplined himself, meditating in the woods. He grew weaker and weaker and felt his mental faculties slipping away. As he neared death from starvation, he was suddenly struck by the fact that he could no longer think and was on the verge of death without having resolved anything. He knew that this extreme path would never lead him to solve life's difficulties, and he should not allow himself to die without succeeding in his quest. Therefore, at this moment he decided to eat and drink to regain his strength. His fellow monks disapproved, offended. This was not the ascetic way. They chastised him and left him alone in the woods. Siddhartha returned to pure meditation, determined to reach understanding. He sat under a Bodhi tree, deep in meditation.

The first night, he was besieged with doubts, agonies, and pains.

He remembered his former life of luxury and was tempted to return to it. But his driving urge to solve the problem of suffering prevented him. As the light of dawn lit the horizon, he underwent a profound enlightenment experience. He felt calm. Answers to the fundamental problems of life seemed clear. At first, he was tempted to remain withdrawn in his own happiness and calm state. Then he felt compassion for humanity and left his seclusion. Beginning in the city of Benares, he traveled around for forty years, speaking, drawing followers to him, communicating his messages to many. Soon even kings were meeting with him to learn to be uplifted, and monasteries were founded throughout India to teach his principles.

He explained to his fellow ascetics, "I remember when a crabapple was my only daily food. I was near death, and yet I came no closer to knowledge." He preached, "Avoid the two extremes, luxury or asceticism. Take the middle path, a path which opens the eyes and bestows understanding, which leads to peace of mind, to higher wisdom, to full enlightenment, to nirvana!" Even today the middle path is a central value in Buddhism. Meditation is the means by which to find it.

Siddhartha discovered the answers to his questions about human suffering. "He who recognizes the existence of suffering, its cause, its remedy, and its cessation has fathomed the Four Noble Truths. He will walk on the right path." The first truth is the recognition that in life, there is suffering—from old age, illness, failures. Second, the cause of suffering is vain, passionate craving. Cravings for being, for nonbeing, for sensual pleasures, and for power are some of the sources of suffering. Third, the cause of suffering can be eliminated by renouncing craving, and finally, the way to accomplish this end is by following the Eightfold Path: right views, right aspirations, right speech, right behavior, right livelihood, right effort, right thoughts, and right contemplation. These doctrines clearly state the lifestyle required.

Siddhartha, who came to be known as Buddha, which means "the awakened one," discovered that enlightenment is the result of what we think. "It is good to tame the mind, which is difficult to hold in and flighty, rushing whenever it listeth; a tamed mind brings happiness." As in Yoga, meditation is central to Buddhism, as a means to conquer the self. According to an ancient Buddhist writing, *The Dhammapada*, "If one man conquers in battle a thousand men, and if another conquers himself, he is the greatest of conquerors." Ethical conduct in life is central in this meditative approach, as are tempering the character, and putting into practice the insights gained from meditation.

Bodhisattva Manjusri Sitting on a Lion
Chinese, Tang dynasty (618–906), coarse white marble.
Gift of Admiral and Mrs. Charles K. Duncan.
San Diego Museum of Art.

As in our Western scientific method, observation is the starting point, but it leads to different conclusions due to the scope of inquiry. Buddha observed that the world is always in a process of changing and eventually deteriorating due to its transitory nature. He said, "Know that whatever exists, arises from causes and conditions and is in every respect impermanent." This includes what we consider our personality, our daily concerns, problems, and worries. Underlying it all is a larger, universal, unchanging reality that includes all things and beings.

Through meditation and renunciation of unnecessary worldly attachments, any sincere seeker can become attuned to the greater reality and thus reach calmness. Illusions from mistaken assumptions obscure the light of insight. Recognition that the distinctions given to things are false can bring enlightenment. In the Surangama Sutra, Buddha pointed out that assigning categories and names to things is like trying to take a pinch of space between your fingers and hold on to it: you cannot. Practitioners must maintain a high level of moral conduct in order to attain clear awareness. Through meditation on the Eightfold Path, negative tendencies are inhibited. Buddha held that people would be bound to the world of illusion and suffering unless they sincerely behaved well toward others. This exemplary behavior is expressed as the classical forms of virtue: no lying or deceit, never stealing, remaining honest and sincere. If people practice such virtue, nothing can hinder them from achieving whole-hearted enlightenment.

BRANCHES OF BUDDHISM:
THERAVADA AND MAHAYANA

Not until sixty years after Buddha's death were his doctrines written down in what are called the sutras. These sutras were passed along through hundreds of generations, and as happens over time, people developed differing interpretations and traditions. By the time of Christ, Buddhism had divided into two major sects. To the north, the Buddhists termed themselves Mahayana, the Greater Vehicle. The sect in the south was called Hinayana, the Lesser Vehicle. The

Hinayanas did not consider themselves a lesser form of Buddhism and so changed their name to Theravada, as it is known today. Over the years, each sect continued to evolve.

Theravada Buddhists have perpetuated Buddha's original, simple, and somewhat austere rules of discipline. The religious seeker, known as an *arhant,* is a saintlike person who lives a monastic life, separate from society. Each person is an individual, capable of enlightenment if he or she follows the way. Theravada Buddhists seek enlightenment through the transcendence of desire. A life of virtue and willpower, with strict adherence to a precise code of conduct, leads the practitioner to buddhahood and enlightenment. Today Theravada Buddhism is practiced widely in Burma, Thailand, Vietnam, and other parts of Southeast Asia.

Mahayana Buddhism expanded on the original teachings of Buddha to include the concept of social responsibility and openness to many means of bringing about enlightenment. The arhant elite saint who reaches high levels of understanding was replaced by the *bodhisattva.* Instead of seeking and being satisfied with personal enlightenment, bodhisattvas set as their goal the enlightenment of the entire world. They choose not to live sequestered in monasteries but to participate in everyday society. They believe that the truly enlightened are compassionate toward others. These Buddhists feel they cannot rest in nirvana until all sentient beings are brought to realization as well. How can they leave others out of their bliss? All beings are part of each other, sharing in the Oneness. A major belief of Mahayana Buddhism is that salvation can be discovered within your everyday life. Enlightenment does not come through denial, detachment, or escape from worldly existence, but in realizing unity with the inner harmony, already present within the ever-changing flux of life. Once people recognize this, they feel a tremendous liberation from obstacles and bondage. Daily life itself becomes divine. This form of Buddhism has become widespread in China.

OTHER FORMS OF BUDDHISM

As Buddhism spread throughout the Eastern countries, many new sects arose. Although each had its creative flavor, they tended to be relatively consistent with Buddhist principles. Zen Buddhism, Tendai, and the Pure Land sect are outgrowths of Mahayana that flourish today throughout the world, even in the United States.

Visualization is most highly developed in the Tantric tradition, but actually all Eastern meditative approaches use it. An image may crystallize a concept. It may then be concise and accessible for meditation. Even a person who cannot read or write can use visualization. The ultimate expression of visualization is a mandala, a diagram symbolizing the central concepts of Buddhism. Mandalas are used for concentration and meditation as a map of the system of constructs. Simpler visualization devices, which we will use in later chapters, help to focus and direct the energies.

❦

The Yogis control the self by controlling the mind. The Buddhists raised the status of the mind to an even higher plane. They believed that people mistake their own deluded conceptions of phenomena for true reality, which causes suffering. Through reasoned meditation with correct concentration, people can gain liberation from every thing conceived. Buddhism encourages us to recognize the great power we have resting within our own minds and to use it well. Meditation is the tool that gives us access to this power.

Scholars Converse on a Bridge by Chen Chou
Chinese, Ming dynasty (1368–1644)
hanging scroll, ink and colors on silk.
Gift of Frederick A. Schafer. San Diego Museum of Art.

3

ZEN BUDDHISM: SEE INTO YOUR TRUE NATURE

A special tradition outside the scriptures
No dependence upon words or letters
Direct pointing at the soul of man
Seeing into one's nature and the attainment of
  buddhahood.

—Bodhidharma

uddhism became complex as it was passed down through generations of patriarchs and interpreters. After more than a thousand years, Buddhism had become an elaborate set of intellectual doctrines, with traditions and rules for every aspect of life. Bodhidharma, who was to become the first Zen patriarch and who was the twenty-eighth patriarch in the direct lineage to the Buddha himself, felt a need to step outside what he believed to be limited and stultifying practices in Buddhism and return to basics. He focused attention on the source of enlightenment, the living, meditative state itself.

Zen is a Japanese word that means "meditation." As a philosophy with a definite approach to meditation, Zen spread from India to China, Korea, Japan, and beyond. The emphasis is on experience of higher truth and reality through direct transmission of insight from mind to mind, irrespective of doctrines, temples, organizations, and rituals. You cannot use analysis to comprehend Zen. Comprehension comes not as the solution to a puzzle but as a realization of what simply is. According to Paul Reps, a Zen scholar, the benefits of Zen come by "grace, not logic." Enlightenment occurs in an instant. Years and years of study in a monastery may prepare and set the stage for it to take place or may paradoxically obstruct the spontaneous experience. Comprehension will occur through the wisdom of intuition. Enlightenment cannot be expressed rationally. It is best communicated through classic stories.

BODHIDHARMA

Bodhidharma was the founder of Zen, which is a sect of Mahayana Buddhism. Legend credits him with being the first to teach martial arts and with bringing tea to China.

According to history, Bodhidharma was born a Brahman prince in the southern kingdom of Pallava in India. When he was very young, he became a student of the great Buddhist master Prajnatara. He was a star pupil who achieved enlightenment rapidly. To recognize Bodhidharma's accomplishments, Prajnatara gave him his religious name, Bodhidharma, which translates as "the Law of Enlightenment." Bodhidharma matured to become a large, dynamic man of character who carried himself with dignity and authority.

After his teacher died, Bodhidharma left India for China to spread the wisdom of his Buddhism. According to legend, he set out alone across the land by foot, a long and dangerous journey. He did not believe in carrying weapons or in killing animals, despite the dangers from bandits and wild animals. He ate vegetables and fruits from the land rather than take the life of an animal. He befriended, observed, and studied animals' natural ways, including how they fought. Practical applications of their methods suggested themselves to him, including how to defend oneself against attack without using weapons.

When Bodhidharma finally arrived in China, he preached his own unique form of Zen Buddhism. At one point during his travels, he was given an audience with Emperor Wu of the Liang Dynasty (502–557), a devout and generous Buddhist. Their dialogue is famous. The emperor asked Bodhidharma, "Many monasteries have I built, many scriptures have I distributed. Many alms have I given, and I have upheld the Faith. Have I acquired merit?"

Bodhidharma, filled with the naive purity of Zen contemplative nothingness, enthusiastically replied, "None."

"In what then does true merit consist?"

Bodhidharma responded with an understanding that is central to Zen: "In the obliteration of matter by absolute knowledge, not by external acts."

Furious with this answer, which negated all his efforts, the emperor banished Bodhidharma from the royal presence in disgrace. Bodhidharma traveled north to Hunan and settled there at the Shaolin Temple. Soon after arriving, Bodhidharma turned to a wall and meditated in silence for nine years! No one could disturb his calm or get his attention. Finally, one worthy disciple among the many who came begged for his teaching and received it. But that is another story.

During long, grueling hours of intense meditation, Bodhidharma, exhausted, sometimes found himself drifting off to sleep. He refused to give in to fatigue. To prevent his eyes from closing, he tore out his eyelashes, which fell to the earth. It is said that from these lashes sprang the first tea plants. Tea became linked to meditation throughout China, then Japan, and later ritual use spread to England and beyond.

After Bodhidharma came out of his meditative trance, he began to help and guide the monks in his form of meditation. He observed that the monks were not learning well and that they were unhealthy due to their inactive lives. He invented a way for the monks to meditate while moving. These original eighteen patterns were written down by Bodhidharma in the *I-Chin-Ching*, which survives as a book today. Movements drawn from these original patterns will be presented for you to try in chapter 10. Over generations of followers, these patterns were embellished, eventually evolving into movements that could be used for many purposes, including martial arts. The Shaolin Temple became known as a center for martial arts training and still is today, in a historically accurate rebuilt Shaolin Temple. Many martial arts consider Bodhidharma their patriarch.

Bodhidharma is remembered as the personification of Zen. His Zen Buddhism spread throughout China, thence to Korea as well as to Japan, and on to the West. Today it flourishes around the world. Certain traditional forms of Zen faithfully follow his traditions. Practitioners even meditate facing the wall. Other Zen sects have used Bodhidharma's teachings as a springboard for their own interpretations. All Zen practitioners are indebted to his dynamic influence.

NOT DOING, NOT THINKING

Even a good thing is not so good as nothing.

—Zen phrase

Once there were three people who took a walk in the country. They happened to see a man standing on a hill. One of them said, "I guess he is standing on a hill to search for lost cattle."

"No," the second said, "I think he is trying to find a friend who has wandered off somewhere."

Whereas the third said, "No, he is simply enjoying the summer breeze."

As there was no definite conclusion, they went up the hill and asked him, "Are you searching for strayed cattle?"

"No," he replied.

"Are you looking for your friend?"

"No," again.

"Are you enjoying the cool breeze?"

"No," yet again.

"Then why are you standing on the hill?"

"I am just standing" was the answer (Yanagi 1972, 123).

Today our lives are usually filled with goals and plans. Rarely do we find ourselves "just standing" like the character in the story. Amid the flurry of activity, human beings strive and search yet lose understanding of life's true meaning. We of the West think of a productive, positive lifetime as busy, always filled, tending toward something purposeful, with goals. Zen offers a creative perspective that can be found by pausing to "stand." This pausing is called readiness or mindfulness. According to Shunryu Suzuki, a highly regarded Zen master who founded the San Francisco Zen Center, "It is the readiness of the mind that is wisdom."

> Nan-in, a Japanese master during the Meiji era (1868–1912) received a university professor who came to inquire about Zen.
>
> Nan-in served tea. He poured his visitor's cup full, and then kept on pouring.

The professor watched the overflow until he no longer could restrain himself. "It is over-full. No more will go in!"

"Like this cup," Nan-in said, "you are full of your own opinions and speculations. How can I show you Zen unless you first empty your cup?" (Reps 1980, 19)

The visitor in this story epitomizes the modern person, filled with opinions on every subject. Zen students first learn to empty their minds of preconceived ideas. This practice of emptying the mind is one of the fundamental types of meditation, which you will learn to practice in later chapters.

Zen seeks meaning from creative experiencing brought about in meditation. In this simple, direct state, the mind is open. The individual is neither striving nor planning but simply "being." Trivial concerns lose their attraction. Each activity becomes an opportunity. Things clarify intuitively, naturally. Bodhidharma expressed this in his typically direct way: "Not thinking about anything is Zen. Once you know this, walking, standing, sitting, or lying down, everything you do is Zen. To know that the mind is empty is to see the Buddha. . . . To see no mind is to see the Buddha."

FIND YOUR TRUE NATURE

The point we emphasize is strong confidence in our original nature.

—Shunryu Suzuki, *Zen Mind, Beginner's Mind*

You must see your original nature. Only you can do it. Searching for answers outside yourself is useless. In "The Wake-up Sermon,"

Bodhidharma defined what he meant by mind and showed how our own mind is the source of enlightenment:

> To search for enlightenment or nirvana beyond this mind is impossible. The reality of your own self-nature, the absence of cause and effect, is what is meant by mind. Your mind is nirvana. You might think you can find a Buddha or enlightenment somewhere beyond the mind, but such a place does not exist.

Bodhidharma was against the use of sutras, prayers, or religious canons to guide people on the path. Rather, he believed that discovering true wisdom is a personal, subtle experience that has no formulas or maps.

The modern Zen way permits practitioners to pursue what they already do with a quality of mind that is Zen. In this way even the most mundane activity becomes a Zen art, and is done with full attention and concentration on being in the moment. Sensory awareness shows practitioners how to awaken themselves through the senses. You will experiment with this in later sections of this book.

Zen also teaches students to achieve an unbroken continuity of awareness through *zazen*, sitting quietly, doing nothing. The ultimate, wordless meditator develops sincerity, naturalness, and complete immersion in whatever he or she does. In the words of Yun-men: "In walking, just walk. In sitting, just sit. Above all, don't wobble" (Watts 1957, 135). Zen recognizes that we live in this world yet need not be limited by its demands. Indeed, we can use every situation to be aware and transcend.

The Japanese samurai took this Zen philosophy to its final

degree. They had to be ready to give their all to every encounter and, if required, to die fearlessly at any moment. Once swords were drawn, there were no second chances. Calligraphy is a nonviolent application of Zen Buddhism. Each stroke of the brush must be exact. Ink cannot be erased.

ONLY YOUR MIND

Bodhidharma believed that people should not be concerned with mere appearances. "All appearances are illusions," he wrote. Like the Buddhists, Bodhidharma saw the transitory nature of everyday concerns and the importance of full commitment to meditation. According to him, only the mind is always present; we just do not realize it. When we get in touch with the mind, we find the source of wisdom.

Bodhidharma helped his disciples to trust themselves as the source of wisdom instead of turning outward away from meditation to find answers to their questions.

"May I hear from you about the Dharma Seal of All the Buddhas?" Jinko asked.

"The Dharma Seal of All the Buddhas is not obtained from another," the Master said.

"Your disciple's mind is as yet without repose," said Jinko. "I beg you, Master, let me have repose of mind."

"Bring me your mind and I will repose it for you," the Master replied.

"Though I seek for my mind, I cannot get it," said Jinko.

"I have reposed your mind for you," said the Master.

At these words, Jinko attained satori [enlightenment].
(Miura and Sasaki 1965, 40)

Problems come from illusions and misconceptions. These same problems dissolve with insight. When you try to seek understanding, paradoxically you lose it. The way cannot be found outside. It must come from within. Enlightenment brings the vision of insight.

The way to prepare for enlightenment is through a paradoxical form of meditation. As soon as you think of trying to empty your mind, your mind is no longer empty. It is self-defeating to try to be natural, just as it is impossible to voluntarily do the involuntary or premeditatively be spontaneous. How does the Zen practitioner reconcile this seemingly impossible situation?

THE KOAN

After Bodhidharma, Zen grew in popularity and spread. Eventually, there were so many students that the famous masters had less time to communicate privately with each one. To accommodate many novitiates at once, they presented groups with a certain question to ponder. These questions eventually became codified into *koans* (which translates as "public record") for all Zen students to solve. Koans offered a method of teaching that sidestepped the need for a creed, precepts, or doctrines. When koans were presented to students, their reactions could be observed and their depth of understanding could be assessed.

In Rinzai Zen, which flourishes today in Japan, students go through a curriculum of koans devised to help them realize the fundamental aim of Zen: to see into one's own true nature. When a student first enters the monastery, he or she is usually given a koan, such as "Listen to the single hand," which is sometimes stated as "What is the sound of one hand clapping?" Another early koan asks: "Has the dog Buddha nature or not?" After their first experience of the flash of insight, students are guided to expand it toward deeper wisdom with the use of koans in sequence, combined with meditation.

The koan presents a puzzling question or problem to concentrate on that does not appear to have any clear answer, especially not a rational, verbal one. Concentrating on the koan has the effect of "stop[ping] the student's word-drunkenness and mind-wandering" (Reps 1980, 111). To the Koreans, who also practice a form of Zen, the koan, or "kong-an" in their language, is seen as an expression of freedom that liberates the mind from its usual restrictions. While there is a long tradition of classical koans and their interpretations, their essence is in their use. Any one specific interpretation is superficial and misleading.

Everyday modes of analysis and thinking do not help to solve a koan. With discipline and continued commitment, Zen monks devote every waking moment to the solution. Insight comes in a flash, often when the meditator least expects it.

Long ago a man once said, "For the study of Zen there are three essential requirements. The first is a great root of faith, the second is a great ball of doubt, the third is great tenacity of spirit. A man who lacks any one of these is like a three-legged kettle with one broken leg" (Miura and Sasaki 1965, 43). To penetrate a koan, practitioners must have faith that within their own intrinsic nature they possess the potential insight needed. Yet without thorough questioning and doubt, seekers will not be able to penetrate the koan. Only with tenacity of purpose will they succeed. The solution is surprising and original, beyond words. Modern Zen practice often is a mixture that includes koan study, meditation practice, and application in daily life. You, too, can add the meditative dimension to your everyday routines and find greater joy in your life.

Empress Chang (Emperor Hung-Chi's wife) Blessed by Taoist Deities (detail) by unknown court painters Chinese, Hung Chi period (1488–1505) handscroll, ink and colors on paper. Gift of Mr. and Mrs. John Jeffers. San Diego Museum of Art.

4

TAOISM: THE WAY
OF HARMONY

Knowing others is wisdom,
Knowing yourself is Enlightenment.

—Lao-tzu, *Tao te Ching*,
chapter 23, trans. by Lin Yutang

T aoism is an ancient philosophy and form of meditation that began in China about the same time that the Greek culture flourished in the West. Taoism looked at the human condition and came up with answers that still make sense today. The truths are timeless and offer a new perspective to modern problems, just as they have done for centuries.

The *Tao te Ching* is considered the foundation of Taoist thought. While only 5,000 words in length, which is around twenty pages, this book has remained a formidable influence on philosophical thought throughout the ages. It is the heart and soul of Taoism. Though seemingly simple in its presentation, this tiny work has been called "One of the profoundest books in the world's philosophy" (Yutang 1942, 579). It has been translated into many languages. There are 350 complete books of commentary on it and many more fragments that have been lost over time. Contained within its pages is the spirit of Asian philosophy, which expresses great wisdom. It offers modern humanity a subtle alternative to our hectic adjustment: sanity, virtue, and wisdom through noninterference with the natural way of things and a calm mind.

Lao-tzu, who is generally regarded as the author of the *Tao te Ching*, was born sometime during the Chou Dynasty. He was a contemporary of Confucius, another great Chinese philosopher. According to legend:

On the fourteenth of September, 604 B.C. in the village of Ch'u Jen in the country of K'u and the Kingdom of Chiu, a woman leaned against a plum tree to give birth to a child. The birth of this extraordinary man was miraculous. He was conceived sixty-two years before when his mother had admired a falling star. After so many years in the womb, he was born with snow-white hair, able to speak and reason. His name, Lao-tzu, means "Old Boy," which reflects these unusual circumstances. (Welch 1965, 1)

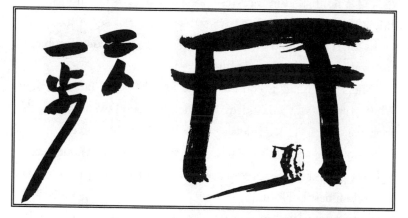

Two People, One Step by Kasumi
Modern work, ink on rice paper. Lao-tzu and the
Gatekeeper leave the *Tao te Ching* behind as they
exit the city, headed for India to convert the
Buddha, never to be seen again.

Lao-tzu became an archivist for the royal court. There he delivered many talks on his philosophy. Ssu-ma Ch'ien, a Chinese historian, recorded that Lao-tzu foresaw the decay and destruction of the dynasty at Le. He decided that he would leave the city by the northwest gate. At the gate, the gatekeeper pleaded with him to write down his views on the Tao and virtue, which he did. These writings became the *Tao te Ching*. He left the book for the people of the city and departed with the friendly gatekeeper, never to return. His death was never recorded. He vanished, although it was claimed that he went to India and converted Buddha to Taoism.

Over the decades Taoism grew in popularity. It became the religion of varied groups of people, from peasants to kings. One Taoist group, known as the "Seven Sages of the Bamboo Grove," were led by Chin K'ang, a poet, scholar, and lute player who lived from A.D. 223 to 262. The Chinese equivalent of beatniks, they lived a free and spontaneous life, gathering in a bamboo grove to meditate, play music, and drink happily. Many became interested in alchemy and developed medicines, paints, and dyes. They are also said to have invented the compass and gunpowder. A group known as the Immortal Sages sought immortality through the Elixir of Life. Some of them reportedly found it and are still living today. Myths and legends about them are recorded throughout Chinese history. These charming accounts communicate the optimism and joy in life that Taoism propagates.

> The mind of a perfect man is like a mirror. It grasps nothing.
> It expects nothing. It reflects but does not hold. Therefore,
> the perfect man can act without effort.
> —Chuang-tzu from *A Source Book in Chinese Philosophy*
> by Wing-Tsit Chan

NO EFFORT

Lao-tzu developed his philosophy in the hopes of stopping the continual conflicts and bitter wars that fragmented his country and wore down the human spirit. According to the *Tao te Ching*, wrongly performed action is the root of many problems. Many passages counsel rulers on how to rule without force or violence, by learning to comply with the natural way of things, in which the interplay of yin and yang will bring balance and harmony.

The concept of yin and yang dates back to antiquity, before written literature. Yin-yang doctrine was an early attempt by Chinese philosophers to work out metaphysics. All reality was understood in terms of a pair of opposites, in tension as dynamic balance. One thing cannot exist without its opposite as background contrast, just as light cannot be understood except in terms of darkness, up without down, good without bad. The idea was further developed to show that not only are the opposites inseparable, but within one there is always a bit of the other. Thus the yin-yang symbol shows the union of opposites, black and white, with a small black dot in the white and a small white dot within the black.

In striving to rule, the ruler sets up counterforces that inevitably come to oppose his rule. Yang conjures up yin, its opposite. Remain in harmony, at one with the Tao, and opposition never arises, Lao-tzu believed. What is there to oppose?

In our modern times, we strive for goals and find ourselves confronted with conflict. We ally ourselves with activities and realms of knowledge, which sets up an automatic adversity between different perspectives. We lose touch with the concrete reality that lies behind our subjective interpretations. Subtly, without quite realizing it, we find ourselves in the midst of conflicts that waste time and divert us from the harmonious path. Taoism advises people to attune to the true nature of what is there and yield to it. By doing so, disputes disappear and solutions to problems suggest themselves. Virtue is the natural state of human beings. It need not be practiced consciously to emerge. Thus the text states:

> Abolish saintliness and reject knowledge: the people will
> benefit a hundredfold.
> Abolish humanity and reject justice: the people will return
> to filial piety and material affection.
> Abolish skill and reject profit: thieves and robbers will
> disappear.
> (Lest) these three be considered as (mere) words which are
> inadequate, let there be something to hold on to.
> Display natural simplicity and cling to artlessness: decrease
> selfishness and diminish desires.
> —*Tao te Ching,* chapter 19, trans. by J. J. L. Duyvendak

Taoism's philosophy of control can be likened to driving a car over ice. If you begin to skid out of control and fight against it by steering the opposite way, the car spins more out of control. If instead you steer in the direction of the skid, going with it, there comes a point when the car rights itself and can be guided back on course. Taoism does not fight against resistance but instead goes with it and utilizes it. By doing so, control is reestablished naturally.

Taoism believes that if you take the path of *wu-wei,* or noninterference, everything begins to make sense. To the Taoists, the true nature of humanity is spontaneously good. While other philosophies, such as Confucianism, seek to train and discipline people, Taoism seeks to bring out the latent goodness in us all. When people are in tune with the Tao, they become virtuous naturally. All people have a tendency to be in balance. The expression "go with the flow" derives from Taoist philosophy. By doing so, confusion and conflict, which can make us feel scattered, hurried, and tense, disappear. Life becomes simpler. Noninterference is the better way for individuals to function. The path of apparent nonaction leads to attunement with the Tao, for the person who is in balance can listen and respond to it.

Who can find repose in a muddy world
By lying still, it becomes clear.
—*Tao te Ching*, chapter 15, trans. by Lin Yutang

The wise person learns to perform "action without deeds," so that all may live in peace. Taoists are not really advocating that we take no action at all, but rather that people take no action that is contrary to nature. Let nature take its course (Wing-Tsit Chan 1963, 207). Then action is transformed due to its source: the Tao. The Taoist seeks unity, the synthesis, rather than becoming too caught up in conflicts, the antithesis. Taoists teach people to live simply, in harmony with the world. We should comprehend ourselves as part of nature and the universe. We can let nature take its course because nature, when allowed to be as it is, will always find the proper balance. If an empty vessel is partially filled with water, the water will always disperse evenly throughout the vessel, taking on its form and finding its own natural level. So also, things left to themselves naturally will tend to resolve as the forces interact.

Reveal thy simple self
Embrace the Original Nature.
—*Tao te Ching*, chapter 19, trans. by Lin Yutang

THE TAO

In early classical writings the Tao is mysterious. Lao-tzu used analogy and metaphorical language to make his point. Later thinkers expressed the concepts through analytical descriptions. Some interpreters see the Tao as the Asian equivalent of God, in that it is all-pervasive, vast, and everything and everywhere at once. However, it would be closer to conceive of the Tao as a manifestation of God, a natural law or way, an order within the universe. The *Tao te Ching* does not address a Supreme Deity directly. Lao-tzu describes the Tao in this passage entitled "The Character of the Tao":

> Tao is empty (like a bowl)
> It may be used but its capacity is never exhausted
> It is bottomless, perhaps the ancestor of all things
> It blunts its sharpness
> It unties its tangles
> It softens its light
> It becomes one with the dusty world
> Deep and still, it appears to exist forever.
> I do not know whose son it is
> It seems to have existed before the Lord.
> —*Tao te Ching*, chapter 4, trans. by Wing-tsit Chan

Taoists believe that our senses mislead us and point us away from the truth. This is not unlike the findings of modern physics, which have shown that what we see is not what is actually there. Modern relativity physics has a parallel theory. The color black, for example, is not a color at all but merely the absence of all colors in the spectrum. White is not a single color but all the colors of the spectrum. Yet we experience white and black as distinct colors, just as we do red, green, and blue. Just as the senses deceive us about reality, the satisfactions of the senses will not satisfy us. The Tao is beyond the senses, an intuition of oneness. We must set aside the usual modes of understanding to truly understand the Tao. Once we do so, guidelines for action come naturally, in keeping with the nature of the Tao.

Looked at, but cannot be seen—
    That is called the Invisible (yi)
Listened to but cannot be heard—
    That is called the inaudible (hsi)
Grasped at, but cannot be touched—
    That is called the Intangible (wei)
These three elude all our inquiries
And hence blend and become one.
        —*Tao te Ching,* chapter 14, trans. by Lin Yutang

The entire thrust of Taoist theory is toward a universal, spiritual principle of which we are all a part and yet which lies beyond us: the Tao. Unlike Yoga and Buddhism, in which people find answers using their own minds, Taoists seek to yield to an experience of unity with the Tao for inspiration and guidance. The Tao is the spiritual way of things, the source of meaning. When people stay with this unity and inner spirit of things, they gain wisdom, sensitivity, and insight.

The Tao brings about the union of opposites, the yin and the yang. Taoists seek balance, seek to include both sides, unified in the wholeness that is the Tao. In this union, there is harmony.

MEDITATION

Meditation is a more appropriate way to understand the Tao than concepts, as we will show you in the following chapters. Meditation flows naturally from the philosophy.

The *Tao te Ching* instructs people on how to approach meditation in the following line:

Can you keep the spirit and body without scattering?
—*Tao te Ching*, chapter 10, trans. by Da Liu

This line encourages people to unify their mind and body through meditation. Unlike Buddhism, Taoism encourages us to be one with our bodies, to make them supple and flexible, so that we can learn to flow with the Tao. This is done by using a special application of the breath to relax the mind and body. When we concentrate on our breathing, we will not be distracted by other thoughts and perceptions. If we breathe carefully and softly, the body relaxes and becomes soft and quiet "like a child."

Can you concentrate your mind to use breath,
Making it quiet as an infant's?
—*Tao te Ching*, chapter 10, trans. by Da Liu

Chuang-tzu (369–286 B.C.), who is considered by many the greatest Taoist philosopher after Lao-tzu, describes breathing that involves the whole body. People usually think of breathing as being just from the lungs or the nose. But in the Taoist conception, breathing is much more. To the Chinese, breathing is linked to the internal energy, or chi. Through the ages, Taoist philosophers have developed theories and techniques of breathing that help to stimulate and direct a person's chi.

Taoist philosophy is concerned with how to maintain energy that will prolong an individual's life and vitality. The forms of meditation attempt to harness internal energy and distribute it, through breathing, movement, and concentration, to all parts of the body. The Taoist objective is healthy longevity. Many of the methods that the Taoists devised are said to improve health, sharpen mental alertness, and add years to one's life, in a practice known as Chi Kung. Some modern martial arts, especially Tai Chi Chuan, use these principles, combined with other ideas, in their practice. Movements are made in unison with breathing, to enhance both the body and the mind. Chinese medicine is based on the circulation of chi and a person's harmonious balance in his or her environment. Breathing is part of this balance.

Chuang-tzu described these whole body breathing techniques: "The breathing of the true man comes deep and silently. The breathing of the true man comes from his heels, while men generally breathe only from their throats" (trans. by Da Liu 1962, 15).

Taoism has given us a different perspective, an alternative set of choices from the typical Western ones. People can learn to let be, unify with the way of nature in the great universal wisdom of the Tao, and thereby live a happy, fulfilled life.

CONCLUSIONS: TRADITIONS IN CONTEXT

Meditation can be thought of as a withdrawing from the world of the senses by removing oneself from the outward-directed intentionality, immersing oneself in the inner world, and refining the experience. The central engagement in all forms of meditation is your experience. Meditation can even help you to contemplate and benefit from interactions, leading to a new synthesis between the inner and the outer worlds.

To us in the West, the self-concept is a vital part of our traditions. Buddhists, however, tend to view the self as an illusion, since actual boundaries between inner and outer, self and not-self, or self and world do not exist; interaction between the two leads to their being inseparable. The Hindus consider the true personal self to be the manifestation of Reality within: the macrocosm within the microcosm. These differences from our Western perspective need not be a hindrance: the experience and the technique of meditation give more insight than the beliefs behind them. In pragmatic terms, if it is useful, then it is valid, as William James, the founder of American psychology, would say.

The rationalist Western perspective promised much. The philosophers of the Renaissance and the Enlightenment were optimistic about the human condition. They came to believe in Science and Reason as the answers to the world's problems. This view of Science is limited, however: Science has yet to integrate its empirical approach to truth with the intuitive truth of natural wisdom. Scientists did not realize that in selecting a certain attitude, they were ignoring the potential insight that is available intuitively. For many people this bifurcation has led to a crisis of faith that continues today. Only in recent years have Westerners begun to delve seriously into the meditative arts for inspiration and relief from rationalism's narrow perspective.

While Eastern traditions offer a great deal to Westerners, often some modification is necessary. Our concept of self and individuality is a driving force in our lives. We are active, assertive, and busily in pursuit of fulfillment. These qualities are positive and should not be given up. Yet we search for more, to help us fill gaps, find deeper meaning, and get more out of our lives. Eastern wisdom's use of focus, yielding, emptiness, and following the middle way can be integrated into our lives through meditation. In the chapters that follow, you will learn the skills to help you find your way along the ancient path of meditation.

PART TWO

Honing Your Meditation Tools

P eople are often ill-equipped to meditate well because they have not been trained in certain mental skills. This section trains you to have better concentration and control over your mind, in preparation for meditation.

5

ATTENTION AND
CONCENTRATION

My experience is what I agree to attend to.
—William James, *The Principles of Psychology*, vol. I

W e can use information from early psychological theory to understand the tools that we will use for meditation, such as attention, concentration, imagination, and visualization. These insights can help you utilize your mental processes to the fullest.

In the early days of psychology, people thought that the mind worked somewhat like a radio. Functioning automatically, it was assumed to receive ideas, just like a radio receives radio waves. One idea linked to the next, by association, to set chains of thought in motion, creating what William James referred to as the "stream of thought." In the mid-nineteenth century, Wilhelm Wundt, the pioneer of experimental psychology, questioned such a simple mechanism. He added attention and perception to this model. His new notion of perception was influenced by Eastern concepts.

Wundt set up the first psychology research laboratory in Leipzig,

Germany. His experiments showed that the mind is not just a passive sensing organ, reacting reflexively to impressions received through the senses. Instead, a compounding of these impressions takes place in the mind, beyond the mere receiving. Once held in the attention, an idea tends to draw other associated ideas together with it in a process Wundt called *apperception*. Apperceptions form a creative synthesis, which evolves. The synthesis is active and dynamic, and can create a unity or whole that is more than the sum of its elements, the stimuli and the mind receiving them. Intelligence and the creative use of the mind are the results of apperception. What is thought interacts with what is perceived through attention and concentration. Attention is the selecting mechanism through which ideas come together in a creative synthesis of apperception. Eastern approaches attempt to set this selecting mechanism aside, to experience directly.

Yogis, Buddhists, and Taoists recognize that our experiencing of the world is not a determined absolute, but results from our thoughts, perceptions, and interactions. They believed—and still believe—that deeper understandings must come through use of the mind. While Wundt's scientific method of research may have differed from the meditative philosophers of the past, both the ancients and the moderns have looked for the source of truth within the human mind.

ATTENTION

Concentration of attention is one of the most essential tools for meditation. Your attention must be focused carefully to direct your mind to what is most important. If you do not concentrate on what is taking place, you may have difficulty experiencing it consciously. Certain learning disabilities, such as "attention deficit disorder," point to the central importance of being able to use attention properly for learning and functioning. When individuals do not concentrate well, their performance suffers, as does their ability to learn. This tendency may be addressed through meditation, which trains the attention. With well-developed attention, memory improves, perception becomes sharper, learning is enhanced, performance is better. Through exercises that concentrate the attention on specific objects, you can bring the faculty of attention under control, developing it more fully for use with meditation. You may then choose to let the attention be free-floating and spontaneous, to go where it wishes, or else to be controlled and deliberate. All intellectual functioning benefits.

ATTENTION TRAINING EXERCISES:
SEEING

Seeing is an important component of attention, but often we are not at one with our experience. For example, while we are looking at something, we might be thinking about something else. Furthermore, our senses often are exhausted by the pace of modern life. We make great demands upon our eyes in both work and play. Many jobs require long hours looking at a computer screen. We strain to read small print sometimes in poor light conditions. For our leisure we spend hours staring at the small glittering screen of a television. Rarely do we think about our eyes unless they become a problem to us. However, eyes, just like other parts of the body, can be relaxed and freed from rigid patterns. Viable methods for training and improving vision were developed and used in Yoga and later rediscovered in other systems. Artists learn to observe as part of drawing and painting. Here we include some exercises that will help you to become more relaxed in your eyes, which will help with attention and visualization skills.

EYE SWING EXERCISE

Stand comfortably, weight balanced evenly between your two feet with hands at your sides. Begin to swing your arms around from one side of your body to the other. Allow your body to twist with your arms, pivoting your feet as well. Let your head turn along with your body. As you make each swing, keep your eyes straight ahead and relaxed, so that your field of vision moves as you move. Your surroundings will seem to rush past you. Do not stop your head from flowing with the movement. After several minutes of pivots, back and forth, your eyes will feel looser.

PALMING

The eyes can become very tired, and this tension carries through your whole body. Palming can relieve and relax your eyes. Sit or lie down comfortably. Close your eyes. Place your palms very lightly over your eyelids. Your fingertips can rest on the top of your forehead. Do not press. Rest for several minutes. Allow your eyes to relax beneath your palms. Let go of any unnecessary tension you might notice in your face.

ATTENTION TRAINING EXERCISES: OBSERVATION

Observation is an important component of attention. Attend to what you see. The experience will lead to development of your mind.

OBSERVATION EXERCISES

One natural way to train the attention can be drawn from your everyday life. Observe the things presented to your senses. For example, go for a walk outdoors in nature—in the woods, a park, the desert, or the seashore. As you walk, look at all the colors you can. Notice the spectrum, with its hues and tones. You may choose to focus on a sense other than the visual—on sounds, for example, or, smells.

Another environment that is readily accessible to most people is the grocery store. Such stores present many objects with intense colors, shapes, smells, and variety. Don't go to make any purchases. Disregard brands, labels, or even what the things are. Instead, notice the colors and patterns, the shapes of the containers, without thinking about them. Next, try using your sense of smell to orient yourself. Each aisle has characteristic odors and arrangements. How does it affect you? There is a close connection between sensory experiences and the emotions. Salespeople know this and use it in their displays. Note how the bright colors of containers, the lettering and packaging shapes, the brightly lit labels or sale tags are designed to catch the attention. Impulse items are located where you can impulsively take them and add them to your cart.

As an interesting variation of this exercise, try going to a supermarket that you have not been to before with a particular item that you want to buy in mind. Note how your attention is affected. As you go about the store, your reactions are

Observation Exercises, continued

changed. You search for the item and discover that there are clear courses to follow. What is your experience of the people and things in the store? A task or project helps to focus the attention, and reaction times are affected. There is not, however, a way to subtract the human factor from the interaction. One's own feelings and point of view matter.

TESTING YOUR OBSERVATION SKILLS

Robert Houdin (the famous French magician of the 1800s from whom Harry Houdini took his name) trained his nephew with this classic exercise. You can test your developing observational skills, while sensitizing your abilities with attention in the process.

Walk into a room, pause briefly for one minute, then leave. Now attempt to describe everything in the room: the objects, the room itself, the atmosphere, the lighting. If you are doing this alone, you may find it helpful to jot down on paper what you remember. Return and compare the actual experience to your remembered one. Again, now, observe carefully. Spend a bit more time: five minutes. Observe carefully. Then leave and describe the room and its contents. Return. How many things do you notice this time? How detailed is your description?

There are many possible variations of this exercise. Are you more intrigued by auditory experience? Try this with an auditory impression. Record a minute of sound from somewhere with a variety of available sounds. Try to recall all that you heard. Play back your recording and compare your experience. You can also perform this exercise using prerecorded music. Try listening to a CD or album that you like, paying careful attention to the details of the rhythm, the bass, the beat, the harmony, the melody, the theme and so on. Then pause the recording and recall as clearly as possible what you heard. Once again, listen to the actual music and compare it to your memory image. This exercise can also be done with a videotape, and scenes or dialogue.

INNER AND OUTER ATTENTION

Attention may be directed to inner or outer objects of consciousness. Classical Zen theorists consider these terms to be meaningless, but from our Western orientation, they help to describe direction. When you notice things about yourself, such as your sensations, feelings, thoughts, or beliefs, your attention is said to be turned inward. When you observe things around you, such as your house, your friends or family, nature or art, you may be said to be attending to the outer. Try the following exercises to understand the concepts more fully. With these two exercises, you begin to learn to take charge of the focus of your attention, first inward, then outward.

INNER ATTENTION EXERCISES

Close your eyes. Sit comfortably. Pay attention to your skin. Does it feel warm or cool or right in between? Where do you notice your temperature most? Can you feel your face? Feel the temperature on your hands and arms. Are there any temperature differences between your face and your arms? Focus your attention on this until you can feel the temperature of the skin in these areas. When you are finished, open your eyes. You may vary this exercise, focusing on different parts of the body, or using other senses, such as weight, comfort/discomfort, tension/relaxation.

Attention may be trained on outer objects as well. First you must select the area to be emphasized. One such outer-focused exercise using art galleries follows. If you do not like art galleries, choose a place or activity that you do enjoy, such as a sporting event, a walk in the woods, or a visit to the mall.

EXERCISE IN OUTER ATTENTION: THE ART GALLERY

Go to an art gallery, of the sort of art that you are drawn to and can appreciate. Walk around and observe the paintings, sculptures, installations, or whatever is presented there. Notice the lines, the colors, the sizes and shapes, the themes the artist is attempting to communicate. The intention to observe is an important component of this exercise. Your perception is sharpened and clarified as you narrow your field of attention. You probably will have an experience of spontaneous attention. You like what you see, so it is easy to concentrate on it. Using spontaneous attention can seem exciting and fascinating, and thus may seem effortless and stimulating. One example of spontaneous attention is getting so involved in reading a book that you cannot put it down until it is finished. A variation of this exercise would be to go to a concert and immerse yourself in what you hear.

SPONTANEOUS VS. DELIBERATE
USE OF ATTENTION

The literature of classical psychology has pointed out that interest and attention are linked. It is easier to pay attention to what we are interested in. Attention may be deliberate or spontaneous, according to William James. What this means in common-sense language is that some objects grab our attention whether we will it or not. Suddenly we find ourselves noticing and then paying close attention to such matters. For example, imagine that you are driving calmly down the road pondering the vicissitudes of life. A fire engine comes racing down the street, its siren blasting, bearing right down on you. You notice it immediately and probably pay very close attention to it as you pull over and get out of the way. This illustrates spontaneous attention. It is sharp, effortless, and immediate.

All of us have experienced the effort needed to stay awake or focused on a boring class or work assignment. This is an example of the use of deliberate attention. "Willpower" is developed, in part, through the discipline of deliberately attending to something that might not capture our interest spontaneously. To some, willpower is a virtue. With practice, it becomes easier to focus attention deliberately. Stilling the mind requires focus.

Both types of attention are useful, depending on the circumstances. The two exercises on inner and outer attention use your capacity for spontaneous attention. The following exercises require that you experiment with the deliberate use of attention.

EXERCISE IN DELIBERATE ATTENTION

Now, to contrast your pleasant experience at your favorite art gallery, visit a gallery with an exhibition that you know will not be particularly interesting to you. (If you choose to do the former exercise at a sporting event, shopping center, or in a natural setting, do this exercise with something that you do not like, such as a sport you don't care for, a store that has merchandise you would never buy, or visit an old industrial site, for those who prefer nature.) As you walk around, notice what it is like to pay attention to what is there yet not really want to. This is deliberate

Exercise in Deliberate Attention, continued

attention. It can be tiring, as every schoolchild who has to do the next day's boring homework and finds that it requires great effort knows. The capacity to have choice with your attention is very useful, especially in meditation.

6

VISUALIZATION AND
IMAGINATION

*When people's eyes are open, they see landscapes in the
outer world. When people's eyes are closed, they see
landscapes with their mind's eye. People spend hours
looking at outer landscapes, but there is just as much to
see in the inner landscapes. The landscapes are different, but they are equally valid.*

—Mike Samuels, M.D., and Nancy Samuels,
Seeing with the Mind's Eye

Meditators must develop the ability to visualize. Visualization, seeing imagery in the mind, is a fundamental skill on
which have been based entire Eastern systems of spiritual
development, such as Tantric Yoga. Guided daydream methods are
used extensively in Europe for therapy and mental development.
Hypnosis uses visualization approaches quite frequently, both for
trance induction and for suggestion. Visualization is widely used
because it is powerful and effective.

Some people are natural visualizers. If we ask them to imagine a
beautiful scene in nature, the image instantly appears. For many others, however, nothing comes to mind. If you have difficulty with visualization, the following exercise will give you an experience of an
automatic visualization based on the laws of perception.

PRELIMINARY VISUALIZATION EXERCISE

Pin or tape a square piece of red or green colored paper to a well-lit, white or nearly white wall. Stand away from it, about seven or eight feet at most. Look fixedly at it for two to three minutes. Pay attention to what you see. Observe closely and do not let your eyes wander from the colored square. After the allotted time, close your eyes. Pay attention to what you see. An image of a square will appear. Observe closely. You can also perform this exercise with a piece of colored paper cut in the shape of a circle.

AUDITORY VISUALIZATION EXERCISE

Your sense of hearing can also leave a sort of "after-image" of sound much like the colored shape on the wall. In this exercise, play a song on the radio, tape deck, or CD. Turn the volume up a little higher than you would normally. Listen intently. Then, midway through the song, turn it off. Close your eyes and listen to the silence. Do you hear the song like an "afterimage"?

The more senses you use to visualize with, the easier and more natural visualizations will become. People vary in how they orient themselves, according to noted hypnotist Milton H. Erickson. For some people, vision best helps them take stock of where or how they are. For others, it is the sense of touch. Still others are most aware of sounds. For this reason, you may find that one sensory modality is easier to use than another. By experimenting with all of these modalities, you hone the mental tools needed for meditation.

SENSORY VISUALIZATION EXERCISE

Here is another way to call forth a visual image, using your motor system responses. Draw an imaginary simple figure with your index finger on your other hand—such as a circle, square, or line. Then close your eyes and imagine the simple figure that you drew. If you would like to be more active, crawl a letter on the floor. Then stop, close your eyes, and imagine the letter. Try this with a circle or a square as well. Rather than moving your entire body, you could substitute a head movement, an arm movement, or a foot movement. Try it on the beach, on a rug, in the grass. Even a partner's back can serve as a "blackboard." Draw a letter or shape on the blackboard with your index finger.

Active, alert seeing is a very important component of visualization. It makes possible what Gerald Manly Hopkins described well in his poetry, a process of taking landscapes and making "inscapes" from their inner design or pattern. In the exercises that follow, you will use your eyes along with your attention to see an aspect of your own "landscape" and turn it into a visual "inscape."

IMAGINARY VISUALIZATION

It is possible to imagine things that are not exact replicas of objects in your environment. Children do this all the time in their play. This exercise can be fun!

Close your eyes. Imagine a two-dimensional shape such as a triangle, circle, or square. Try to visualize it, with a definite size and color. Allow it to become larger and larger until it appears huge. Next, let it become smaller and smaller until finally it is so small that all you can see is a single dot. One variation is to change its shape, for example, from a circle to a square. Keep control. Open your eyes when you are finished.

OBJECT VISUALIZATION

Choose a simple, ordinary object you use in daily life, such as a cup or vase, a ball, a flower. Place it on the floor and sit down next to it. Look at it for two to three minutes. Notice everything about how it looks. Next, move to the opposite side and look at it from another perspective. Move closer to the object and inspect the details. Notice colors, textures, and how the light strikes it. After you feel that you have observed this object thoroughly, close your eyes and try to visualize it. Usually an image of it will appear in your mind. It may be very vague, just a glimmer, or extremely clear and distinct. If nothing appears in your mind, open your eyes and observe the object again. Repeat the process several times until you are able to have an accurate image and retain it. Remember, visualization is a natural capacity of the mind. Discovering how to experience and direct it may take some practice.

PASSIVE IMAGERY EXERCISE

The visualization exercises you have tried are samples of active visualization, where you give yourself an image to see in the mind's eye. Next we experiment with passive visualization, which taps into the unconscious mind. To work with your mind in this way, you take a more wait-and-see attitude. Be curious about what you will experience; curiosity and wonder open your mind so that you may receive new data.

In the early 1900s, Hans Silberer, a German psychiatrist and theorist, found he could solve complex problems by using his inner mind. He did his experiments when he was in what he called the "twilight state," the drowsy, or hypnagogic, state between sleeping and waking: at that time attention drifts and the body is relaxed. He discovered that if he presented himself with a problem to solve and then waited, his mind would offer him a meaningful image that symbolized the solution. Many famous scientists, artists, and writers have drawn from the wellsprings of the inner mind for creative inspiration. Inner symbolic imagery comes to mind spontaneously and later can be consciously contemplated to determine its meaning.

This imagery is known as "hypnagogic" because it takes shape just below the threshold of the conscious mind. Often, because hypnagogic images reach deep into the psyche, such imagery is very important and personally meaningful.

Hypnagogic images are often deeply symbolic. They put together and communicate many aspects of something into one meaningful, unified picture. This capacity of the mind to find understanding symbolically has been used for millennia. Tibetan Buddhists have created elaborate mandalas, rich with symbols, in order to understand a higher reality. You can use your capacity to visualize and symbolize to develop your creativity and help you solve problems. The following exercises guide you in developing these skills.

EXERCISE IN PASSIVE VISUALIZATION

In order to experience hypnagogic imagery, you must put yourself into a situation where it is likely to occur. Close your eyes. Invite your mind to have an image. Do not be specific. Be patient, then wait. The image may arise in the evening, when you are tired, just before sleep, while listening to music late at night, or while sitting in a car while someone else is driving on a long trip. The key to passive visualization is to wish for an image generally, in an invitational sense. You do not push or dictate to yourself with a definite set of instructions, but rather allow an image of significance to come in an open-ended manner. Then it will. As a variation, after a long drive, observe your inner images as you lie down to rest. You may feel imagined motion as well.

Visual thinking is natural and can be very helpful for problem solving. Modern video games use this concept for entertainment. The capacity to reason intuitively through imagination and visualization can be developed through meditation. The following exercise will help to develop and guide this.

DA VINCI'S DEVICE

Leonardo da Vinci created this exercise to teach the mind how to create inventively through imaginative seeing. In allowing his mind to wander creatively, he stimulated his visual imagery.

Look at a wall that has cracks, chips, and paint stains. Let your imagination wander. Notice resemblances to shapes of animals, landscapes, or whatever you see.

UNLOCK PATTERNED VISUALIZATIONS

Architecture students who are training their minds to see their world more creatively perform this exercise. For their training, they also draw their creations on paper. You may or may not want to draw what you imagine. It is your choice.

Take an ordinary object, such as a fan, box, bowl, book—anything. Imagine that you slice it into a number of parts, then put the parts back together in a totally new way. Do not worry about the function of the new object. Let yourself play with ideas. If you like to draw, sketch your ideas as well.

7

THE UNCONSCIOUS MIND

It really doesn't matter what your conscious mind does because your unconscious automatically will do just what it needs to.

—Milton H. Erickson, *The Collected Papers*, vol. I

 ou have practiced attending to what you are aware of, to what you can visualize and imagine, but you may not have considered learning to attend to what you are unaware of. Most of the exercises presented up to this point have involved conscious awareness. Yet another part of the mind can be a positive resource for meditation: the unconscious.

Learning how to attend to the unconscious is somewhat paradoxical, because once you are aware of the unconscious, it becomes conscious! However, you can learn to develop a kind of accepting openness. Then you can attend to your unconscious, letting it be, without interfering, to deepen and extend the range of your mind. The parallel with Zen is clear.

Many people ask, rightly, what the unconscious is and how they can recognize it. The following exercise is designed to help you recognize your unconscious by analogy.

CONSCIOUS VS. UNCONSCIOUS

Imagine that you are sitting in your car in front of some train tracks at a crossing, waiting for the signal, watching. A train slowly approaches from the distance. It grows closer and closer and then begins to pass. It is very long. You hear the *clack, clack, clack* of the wheels on the track. You watch the cars as they pass. Each one is different; some are passenger cars, others carry cargo. While you notice spaces between the cars, you can barely see the background behind the cars. It is a flicker, a view that appears for a split second and then is gone yet is still there again to be perceived, between the next cars. When you focus your attention on that space, however, your awareness of it becomes clearer while the passing cars become the background to your field of attention.

This background behind the cars, which can be glimpsed, is like the unconscious. Think of the cars as the conscious sensations, feelings, and thoughts in the mind, stretching across the horizon. The view glimpsed between the rhythmically spaced boxcars as they pass is the content, what is unconscious. For example, while you are reading this book, you probably are not noticing your foot. But as soon as we mention it, your attention turns to your foot and you notice it and wonder about any sensations there. You might even wonder why we drew your attention there. These and other thoughts and experiences remain unconscious until you attend to them. You can learn to use these unconscious experiences for meditative states. Hypnosis has developed the use of the unconscious to help with clinical problems. For more detail on this, see our book *Principles of Self-Hypnosis* (1991).

When attention is withdrawn from the conscious level of the mind, it does not merely become inattention. Freed to the inner world, it can wander freely and make connections possible. "Evenly poised," "free-floating"—these are the qualities of attention when creatively directed to the inner world. Frequently, people are surprised by the unconscious process. Pleasant new discoveries often occur.

To explore inwardly, attention must be released from rigidly focused selective concentration. In this way discovery and creativity occur. Attention should be turned like a searchlight, randomly, until an interesting association or impression comes to light. This is free-floating attention. Then the attention may be selectively concentrated on it to light it up, like a spotlight. This involves concentration. It is the same with meditation, especially when exploring topics of profound significance.

Now that you have become aware of the unconscious level of thinking, here is another experiment that will help you become sensitive to this aspect of mind. Later, in the meditation exercises, we use these skills and develop them more fully.

EXERCISE IN UNCONSCIOUS RESPONSE

Sit in a supportive chair, with your hands resting either on your knees or on the arms of the chair. Close your eyes. Relax for a moment. Then notice your hands (as you keep your eyes closed). Attend to the feelings in your hands. They might seem to be cool or warm, light or heavy. Wait for the experience to occur. Some people might find that one hand becomes heavier than the other, warmer, or even tingly. Any of these sensations are communications from your unconscious mind. Consciously, you do not know what your hands will feel like as you wait, until you experience the spontaneous response. These surprises come from the unconscious.

UNCONSCIOUS SUGGESTION USING VISUALIZATION AND IMAGINATION

From earliest recorded times, Yoga has used unconscious visualizations as a means of positive suggestion. Self-hypnosis also uses suggestion to evoke unconscious visual imagery for many fascinating experiences.

Visualizations held vividly in the mind tend to engage the ideomotoric sensibility, where the idea (*ideo*) tends to find expression in the action systems of the body (*motor*). The link is made through a fundamental phenomenon: suggestion. Suggestion is the process through which an idea, image, thought, or feeling can activate other processes without effort. Through suggestion, you can get in touch with your normally involuntary abilities and activate new possibilities. Suggestion works through the unconscious mind because its mechanisms often occur automatically, without conscious, rational thought. It is valuable for meditation, where it has been used for centuries. The exercises included here will help you learn to recognize and work with suggestion through linking visualization with motoric sensations.

EXERCISE IN SUGGESTION USING VISUALIZATION

Find a comfortable place to sit, then close your eyes. Imagine a very pleasant experience, a time when you felt very relaxed. Now think about a very tart lemon. Imagine the taste, the smell of lemon, its yellow color. Picture it as clearly as you can, especially remembering the tart taste. Wait.

Do you find your mouth producing extra saliva? Your body produces this automatic response in reaction to your visualization of the lemon. If another taste, perhaps of your favorite food, appeals to you more, feel free to indulge your imagination. You will learn to develop this ability even further in later chapters.

THE CHEVRAL PENDULUM

Ideomotor theory draws upon the kind of experience you developed in the last exercise, the ability of the mind to suggest an experience to which the body responds automatically, thus the name *ideomotor*, which refers to the phenomenon itself. An idea when fully accepted by the mind can be automatically translated into a motoric, body response. The classic exercise in ideomotor phenomena is called the Chevral Pendulum. You can experiment with it now.

EXERCISE IN IDEOMOTOR RESPONSE

Get a plumb bob, heavy nail, metal ring, or any small, heavy object. Attach a string to it. Hold the string from the top and let the object dangle freely. Support your elbow on a table so that you are comfortable as you hold the string, but leave your arm and wrist free. Now close your eyes. Imagine that the pendulum begins to swing back and forth. Picture it vividly in your mind. Do not deliberately move or interfere with the hand that holds the string. Instead, focus on your imaginative image of swinging. Visualize the rhythmic sweep of the swing becoming longer. After a few minutes, open your eyes and look at the pendulum. Most people will find that it is swinging back and forth.

Now close your eyes again. Imagine that the object begins to swing in the other direction. Exaggerate the image so that the arc becomes larger and larger in the new direction. Picture it as vividly as possible. Once again, do not disturb the hand that holds the string. Simply focus on your visualization.

Exercise in Ideomotor Response, continued

After a time, open your eyes. Is the pendulum swinging in the new direction?

Close your eyes one last time. Imagine that the pendulum swings in a circle. Allow the circular orbit to become larger and larger. Open your eyes to check. This may take time and practice to develop further. Some people can do it almost immediately. Others expand their abilities over time. Practice every day or so to develop skill.

The relationship you develop with your unconscious through these exercises will help you in many ways. Meanwhile, enjoy the fun of these experiments. Ideomotor and ideosensory responses will be used in later chapters.

The unconscious mind is a reservoir of potential. Meditation can help you to tap this resource. The meditations in Part Three will guide you along the path.

8
THE MIND-BODY
LINK

*What we call "body" cannot be considered apart from
the rest of the human being. Without the body, we could
not move or think or create. What we call "body" is
ourselves.*

—Betty Keene, *Sensing, Letting Yourself Live*

Meditation can be initiated through the mind or through the
body. You can learn to direct your attention to your body,
just as you learned in earlier chapters to direct your attention to other phenomena. You can choose to approach meditation
with your body or your mind. The mind and body are linked, each
having influence upon the other. You have experienced this through
the ideomotor exercises in the last chapter. When you turn your
attention toward your senses, a shift occurs that gives you new
answers.

Some people are naturally more aware of their bodily experiences than others. You may wonder how you will know when your
muscles are relaxed. The answer is that you can feel a different sensation in relaxed muscles. The following exercises will help you to
develop relaxation skills that you will use in some of the later meditation exercises.

BODY AWARENESS EXERCISES

Just as you can relax your mind, you can also relax your body. The next exercise will help you to relax through your body. These techniques have been used for thousands of years in Hatha Yoga. If you follow all the instructions as best you can, you will find that your body relaxes more fully and that you gain more control over tension. While you can learn to relax specific areas of your body, it may be easier to start with the general, as in this exercise.

BODY RELAXATION

Lie down on your back on the floor, a supportive bed, or a couch. Close your eyes. Rest for a moment. Wait for a feeling of readiness. When you feel ready to begin, tighten all your muscles throughout your body. Tighten the muscles of your face, eyes, mouth, neck, shoulders, arms, legs, stomach, back, front—every area you can think of. Never tighten to the point of discomfort, but do contract your muscles. Hold for thirty seconds. Pay close attention to the sensation. Then let go all over, allowing your muscles to relax. Compare the feeling you have in your muscles now with how your muscles felt when tensed. After a minute or so, contract your muscles a second time. Hold them for thirty seconds, then relax even more fully than the first time. Tense one more time and then relax. Go back over areas of tension to release them. When you loosen your muscles for the final time, your whole body will be able to relax much more deeply. Try to let go of any residual tightness. Take a few moments to enjoy this deep relaxation.

BODY AWARENESS

Lie on the floor so that you feel comfortable. Close your eyes. Scan through your body with your awareness. Do not use your eyes; sense the feeling, without imaginatively looking. If you notice any muscles that are unnecessarily tight, can you let go of the tension? If not, do not fight it. Let it be, with awareness and acceptance, but notice that the tension is there. Breathe comfortably. Take a moment to pay attention to your shoulders. How far is it from the point of one shoulder to the other shoulder? Don't move them. Instead, try to notice the length with your awareness of sensation. How far is it from the tip of your shoulder to the bottom of your fingertips? How long are your legs? How much space do your legs take up? Can you notice your length, from the top of your head to your toes? Continue to scan through your body and make any other observations that occur to you. When you feel ready, sit up, open your eyes, and look around, stretching and moving. Then stand. How do you feel?

People often look outside themselves for happiness and fulfillment. Usually they are disappointed that they do not find it there. Your own inner experience is a source of happiness and strength. It can help you rediscover inner resources that are always with you but are often ignored. Once you have performed the following exercises several times, you may find it easy to turn your attention to your inner experience at different points throughout the day. Eventually, you may notice a deeper attentiveness to your daily activities. Zen monks can find enlightenment in the simplest tasks by being fully aware in every moment of daily life, sitting, standing, and in actions beyond.

FIND YOUR BALANCE

We all live on the earth under the influence of the earth's gravity. When you are aligned with gravity, standing, walking, and running become easier. But how can we tell when we are aligned? Simply standing straight upright is not the answer. This exercise will help you find your balance.

Stand, legs apart at a comfortable distance for you, feet flat on the ground, hands at your sides, head upright, eyes fixed ahead, at ease. Now, rock gently back and forth, forward and back, on the balls of your feet, then the heels, back and forth, forward and back, on the balls of your feet then the heels, to the point of almost losing your balance each time. Concentrate on your sensations. Slowly reduce the sway, until you find a point at which you are centered, at ease, not rocking but still. Now move the same way to each side; gently rock slowly so that your weight shifts first to one foot, then to the other. Gradually reduce the motion until you find a point in the center of stillness. You have sensed your way into an exact balance point, where your body is best aligned with gravity. Repeat the exercise several times until you feel truly comfortable with the center point. If possible, let go of any unnecessary tensions. Enjoy this position for a few moments and then move on to the next exercise.

STANDING

Stand with your feet approximately shoulder-width apart. Close your eyes. Pay attention to how your feet relate to the surface on which you stand. Do you feel as if you press down on the floor, or is it pressing up on you? Does it feel hard, soft, warm, cool? Are you standing with your whole foot, leaning back on your heels, or leaning forward on your toes? There are many possibilities, as you experienced in the previous exercise. Now focus all your attention on standing and nothing else. Do not label the experience with words. If you do find yourself using words, try not to limit yourself to just words. Reach into the experience to become it. Just be standing. When you feel ready, open your eyes.

SITTING

Meditation has traditionally been done in a sitting position. Zen considers sitting itself a meditation. In this exercise, you will find a comfortable, natural way to sit on the floor and focus your attention on the sitting.

Sit on the floor cross-legged. Let your arms rest on your knees and close your eyes. Rock back and forth gently so that you feel your sitting bones under you. Experiment with positioning until you feel comfortable. Now pay attention to your upper body. Sit straight enough so that you can feel balanced and allow your breathing to flow freely. Notice where your head is in relation to your body. Once you have found a comfortable position, sit without moving for several minutes. Practice over a period of time until you can sit for five minutes. This will prepare you for many of the meditations that follow.

ARM LIFT

You can apply the meditation principles to movement. Later you will have the opportunity to apply these skills to enhance sports performance. This exercise will teach you how to focus on movement.

Sit comfortably. Let your muscles relax. Lift one arm slowly out from your side. As you do this, notice which muscles engage to help lift your arm. Feel your skin. Is it warm or cool? Now lower your arm again, slowly. Notice any feelings in your arm and hand. Lift each arm slowly up and down in turn several times, concentrating on the details of the motion.

Zen students meditate to quiet their
minds at the Providence Zen Center.

PART THREE

Taking the Path
of Meditation

It is no matter; in the mind set free
There is no-wavelet dancing on no-sea!
No-Self to tell no-self it shall not be!
Only the dancing pier, the happy wave and me!
—Christmas Humphreys, from "Brighton Pier"

The chapters on attention, visualization, the unconscious, and
the mind-body link have introduced many skills for you to
learn. By practicing the exercises, you have built a foundation for
the meditations that follow. As you work with your mind in meditation, you will find that these abilities interact and overlap in new
and creative ways.

As you embark on the meditative path, it is important not to
become lost in the mechanics. The artist who created the painting
on the cover of this book has devoted much of her life to painting. She explained to us that during her years in art school, she
studied many painting techniques and styles. She emulated the
Old Masters and strove to learn the methods presented. Upon
graduation her professor said to her, "You have learned well. Now
forget everything you learned and just paint!" With these words
of inspiration she developed her own creative style. Though based

on her technical expertise, what she has developed transcends any one style: it is unique. Meditation flows naturally from your own individuality. Let yourself enjoy the exercises as you begin a wondrous journey with your mind.

PRELIMINARIES TO MEDITATION

The place where you choose to meditate can have an effect on your meditation. Most people have been inside a church or temple. The atmosphere within is noticeably different from the outside. When you walk in and sit down, you might notice that people whisper, the quality of light is altered by stained glass or indirect lighting, the air smells sweetly of incense. The atmosphere is calm, quiet, usually conducive to inner exploration.

Try to find a place or places for your meditation where you feel comfortable turning your attention inward. Find an area in your house, outdoors, a church, temple, library, or any other place where you can have quiet, undisturbed time. Is the atmosphere conducive to focused concentration? Choosing a place where you feel comfortable can help you to focus. However, do not go to the other extreme, searching for the perfect place. Meditation is not tied to time or place.

The exercises that follow can be done sitting or lying down. Some people like to sit in a comfortable chair while others prefer to sit on the floor. Occasionally we will ask you to stand. Remember that there are no exact rules for position; the important thing is that you feel comfortable.

As you progress in meditation, you will find more meaning in the experience. Your intuition will become available at times. Learn to recognize and use it. Not all intuitions are infallible, but they can be a valuable source of insight. The unconscious speaks through intuition, and rational faculties do not always capture or explain this. Meditation will help you to develop your intuitive faculties.

9

BREATHING

The mind directs the breath, letting it sink down,
thereby penetrating even the bones.

—Yu-Seong Wu, *Classics of T'ui Chi Ch'uan*

reathing is a physiological process that we all perform naturally, without thought. Traditionally, this seemingly simple body function has been a primary pathway to meditation. Breathing is used in Yoga, Buddhism, Zen, and Taoist meditation as a stepping-stone to the deeper self. Meditative breathing can be linked to many meaningful benefits. Concentration on the breath is a doorway to deeper meditative practices. By meditating on your breathing, you can enhance your calmness, improve your health, and clear your consciousness of extraneous thoughts and concerns.

BREATHING MEDITATION 1:
USE INNER ATTENTION TO COUNT YOUR BREATHS

Sit in a comfortable position. Close your eyes. Count your breaths from one to ten. One complete breath begins with an inhalation and ends with an exhalation. Keep your breathing natural as you inhale and exhale normally. Do not hyperventilate, forcing yourself to take unnaturally deep breaths, or hold your breath. To the best of your ability, try not to think about anything else but your breathing. Count complete breaths after each exhalation: breathe in, breathe out—one. Breathe in, breathe out—two, and so on, to ten. Then begin again with one and repeat. After you are done, open your eyes and stretch. If you would like, you may repeat this exercise at the same sitting. With practice, you will be able to count your breaths without interruption for as long as you would like. Variations may suggest themselves, such as just counting exhalations.

BREATHING MEDITATION 2: CONTROLLED BREATHING

This breathing meditation is drawn from Yoga practices. The Yogis believe this simple and direct exercise to be very beneficial. Sit up straight but not strained, so that your breathing passages are clear. Take your pulse gently by pressing lightly with your fingers at the inner wrist near your thumb. Close your eyes. Breathe in slowly to a pulse count of four. Hold the breath for one pulse beat and then breathe out again, slowly, to a count of four. Hold for one pulse beat and then begin again. Do this without forcing, yet keep control. Relax as you breathe. Do not rush. Do this for a few minutes or so if you are comfortable. Stop if you are not. You can work up to a longer breath: inhale six beats, hold for three, exhale six, hold for three and repeat. Find a comfortable count and maintain it.

BREATHING MEDITATION 3: FOLLOW THE BREATH

Sit in a comfortable position and close your eyes again. This time you will pay careful attention to the process of breathing and follow each breath as it goes in and out. Try to focus all your attention on the sensations from air as it enters into your nose, then down into your bronchi, filling your lungs, and then out through your nose. You will begin to find a natural rhythm as you follow your breath, in and out, in and out, meditatively. Do not interfere with this; simply try to allow it. It may want to change as you relax in this exercise.

Meditations such as counting and following the breath can help you to become more in tune with your natural rhythms. We often overlook many natural rhythms in our busy schedules. One simple rhythm that you can observe as you meditate is the natural cycle of swallowing. In deep meditation, reflexes are slowed. Also, your rhythms will vary at different times of the day, regardless of changes in the room or environment. You probably have noticed cycles of tiredness and wakefulness: at certain times of the day you are at your best in alertness; at other times you may not be very alert. Determine your individual cycles and meditate at your peak moments if possible. Your cycles will form patterns that you can observe. Realize that these patterns may be affected at times by the amount of sleep you may have had, your nutrition, workload, or emotional distress. In Eastern medicine, the vital energy known as *chi* is believed to circulate in twenty-four-hour cycles through the body. Taoism teaches us to find greater harmony with these natural rhythms. All of these different rhythms affect your consciousness. When you stop fighting against your rhythms, you will find greater vitality.

The first step to cooperating more with your inner rhythms is to become aware of them in meditation, as you did with your breathing. You may need to meditate at several points throughout a day, or over several days, to find your pattern. Permit your own individuality, but practice regularly. You will find that you develop a more comfortable harmony with the patterns of your inner self.

BREATHING MEDITATION 4: RELAXING BREATH

Lie on the floor on your back. You can raise your knees and place your feet flat on the floor if this feels more comfortable for your lower back. Place your hands lightly on your solar plexus at the rib cage. Do not press; simply allow your hands to rest comfortably. Close your eyes. Allow your breathing to find its natural rhythm, as you did in the earlier exercises. Pay attention to your breath as it goes in through your nose, down into your lungs, and then out again. Notice the feeling of your rib cage and solar plexus. Can you feel your diaphragm move as you breathe? Do your ribs raise and lower with each breath? How far does your breath travel? Does it fill your rib cage and move lower? Do you feel any chronic tension in your rib cage? Can you let go of any tensions you sense, in your rib cage, chest, or any other related area? If you can relax further, does your breathing become fuller or more complete? Do your rhythms change? After several minutes, or whenever you feel ready, sit up and stretch a bit. You may feel relaxed and refreshed.

Tiger by the Pine by Yokoku
Japanese, early nineteenth-century
hanging scroll, ink and color on silk.
Bequest of Hortense Coulter. San Diego Museum of Art.

10
VISUALIZING

*All that we see are our visualizations. We see not with
the eye, but with the soul.*

—Samuels and Samuels, *Seeing with the Mind's Eye*

BECOMING AN IMAGE

There is an ancient legend of a king in China who commissioned a renowned painter to paint a tiger for him. The painter was invited to do the work in the castle and was given a large, luxurious room. The painter agreed but requested that the king leave him alone to do the work. The king agreed. Once alone, the painter set out his paints, hung the canvas, and then sat in meditation. At dinnertime, the servant brought the painter his dinner. The canvas was empty. The painter did not stir, lost in deep meditation. The next day, the servant returned with each meal, and every time he entered he saw the painter sitting quietly, still meditating, next to a blank canvas.

A week passed. The king became impatient and decided to pay the painter a visit. He found the painter meditating quietly. Another week passed, and another. Finally, the king would wait no longer. He stormed into the painter's room and yelled in his most commanding voice: "If you do not have the painting finished by tomorrow at sundown, off with your head!" But the painter kept meditating.

The next day, promptly as the sun slipped below the horizon, the king entered the painter's room, followed closely by his royal executioner, sword in hand. There on the canvas was the most exquisite painting of a tiger the king had ever seen. The painter smiled and bowed respectfully. The king expressed his pleasure with the work and then asked, "Why, painter, did you wait so long to begin?"

The painter replied simply, "You asked for a magnificent painting of a tiger. I meditated until I became the tiger. Only then could the painting flow naturally."

The king understood the significance and asked if the painter would take him on as a student of meditation, which he did.

This story illustrates the spirit of the following meditation. You will use your imagination and focused mind for an exceptional experience.

IMAGERY MEDITATION I: BECOME ONE WITH THE IMAGE

Sit or lie down comfortably. Pick something you like. People often choose something from nature, such as a tree, flower, or favorite animal. Close your eyes. Vividly imagine the object that you have chosen. Picture it clearly, but do even more: actually experience being the object. For example, if you have chosen a tree, imagine how it feels to be a tree, the wind in your branches, the sunlight on your leaves. Let your body move as a tree moves on a windy day. Let yourself flow with the experience and enjoy it. When you feel finished, open your eyes and stretch.

INTERNAL ENERGY

The Taoists developed the concept of internal energy, which they called *chi*, similar to the *ki* of the Koreans and Japanese philosophies, and prana in Yoga. The West has a corresponding conception in the word *pneuma*, from the Greek. The idea of energy flowing throughout the body is becoming widely accepted today. This energy is the basis for acupuncture, internal martial arts such as Tai Chi, and many forms of holistic healing. Chi is an invisible form of energy, related to the life force, that circulates throughout the body through channels called meridians. Meridians are not veins or arteries, but pathways covering the entire body. Physical processes in the body have corresponding patterns of energy flow. Energy is just as significant as organs, blood, and tissue. Meridians are the pathways that the chi follows.

It is believed that the mind can control the flow of chi. With special exercises, you can learn to access your internal energy and direct it to specific areas. This results in greater vitality and strength as well as more suppleness and flexibility. People who are skilled in controlling their chi can direct their energy to help heal and energize the body. According to traditional Chinese texts, meditations on internal energy add healthy, active years to life. In a recent study performed at a nursing home by Skip Alexander (1989), twelve patients were taught meditation. A control group did not meditate. After two years, eleven of the twelve meditators were healthier, while half of the non-meditators had died. Perhaps meditation really does enhance longevity, as the Taoists claim! In the following meditations, we will work with chi, the positive, vital energy.

MEDITATION 1: VISUALIZE INTERNAL ENERGY

Lie down on the floor or on a supportive couch or bed. Close your eyes. Allow your body to relax. As you breathe in, imagine that the air you draw in flows through you, nourishing your body with needed air and energy. Picture or sense a flow of energy that moves throughout your body, recharging you as you breathe. It flows through your arms, legs, torso, and head. You may experience a slight warming or tingling. While the feeling is subtle, you can experience it if you sensitively try to notice it. Relax any tense muscles, as they tend to block the flow of chi. When you feel finished, sit up, refreshed and revitalized.

MEDITATION 2: RAISE YOUR INTERNAL ENERGY

This exercise derives from an original pattern created by Bodhidharma. It helps to enhance the flow of chi to the extremities.

Stand with your arms hanging down by your sides. Close your eyes and focus your attention on your hands. Allow your arms to be relatively straight but not rigid. Remain relaxed (Figure 1). Keeping your arms somewhat relaxed at the elbow, hands open, palms facing down, raise your arms to shoulder height in front of you as you inhale slowly (Figure 2). Breathe naturally as you lift your arms and concentrate on the sensations. Breathe out as you slowly lower your arms, continuing to concentrate (Figure 3). Do this several times slowly. Do not take forced deep breaths. Rather, keep your breathing comfortable and natural.

Next, raise your arms up at your sides as you inhale (Figure 4), then push slowly outward and exhale gently (Figure 5). Bring your arms in and repeat several times; remain as relaxed as you can be. Don't hunch your shoulders; simply push slowly and smoothly.

Figure 1

Figure 2

Figure 3

Figure 4

Raise your arms slowly over your head with your palms facing up and breathe in (Figure 6). Breathe out as you push upward (Figure 7), then in again as you lower your arms. Repeat several times.

Now bend your arms at the elbows, your hands in front of your chest, palms facing forward. Then step forward with one foot into a front-facing stance (Figure 8). Extend both arms forward, palms flat (Figure 9). Retract your hands back to your chest and then let them drop slowly to your sides as you step back to feet parallel, into a relaxed natural stance. Use the same breathing rhythm as before: breathe out gently as you step out and push, breathe in as you retract your hands

Figure 5

Figure 6

Figure 7

Meditation 2: Raise Your Internal Energy, continued

and drop them slowly to your sides. Now step out with the other foot and push forward with both hands as you step. Return to the natural, even stance.

Now pay attention to your body. Do you feel a warmth

Figure 8   Figure 9

or tingling in your hands, palms, neck, shoulders, or arms? Allow this feeling to spread. When you are ready, open your eyes. Do this exercise regularly, and you will find that eventually you will develop more tingling and warmth. This sensation is related to your internal energy.

MEDITATION 3: VISUALIZE A BALL OF ENERGY

Sit cross-legged on the floor, rug, or grass for this exercise. Imagine that you are holding a large beach ball filled with energy in your lap (Figure 10). Place your arms around and over the top, hands toward the sides of this imaginary beach ball. Relax your arms. Close your eyes and concentrate on the ball of energy touching your arms and hands. Does a tingling begin to develop in your hands? Does the energy help to hold your arms up comfortably? Concentrate, breathe naturally, vividly imagine. Take a few minutes to permit the effects to develop. Then open your eyes.

Figure 10

11
MIND AND BODY IN HARMONY

Through becoming conscious we have been driven out of paradise, through consciousness we can come back to paradise.

—Heinrich Jacoby

B uddhist monks and Yogis have long been able to control many involuntary bodily functions such as heartbeat, pulse rate, and body temperature. You can begin to work with these phenomena and gradually learn to alter these functions through meditation. Doing so demonstrates the direct link between mind and body: boundaries need not be barriers.

MEDITATION 1: TO SENSE YOUR HEARTBEAT

Normally we do not have to remind our hearts to beat. The process takes place automatically, without thought. The unconscious mind controls this and many other bodily functions quite naturally. In this exercise you will activate your unconscious mind using suggestion to become more in touch with one of these automatic processes: the heartbeat.

Lie on the floor or on a comfortable but firm couch or bed. Close your eyes and scan through your body. Turn your

Meditation 1: To Sense Your Heartbeat, continued

attention to your heartbeat. Can you feel your heart beating? Notice the quality of the heartbeat. Is it slow, quick, rhythmical? Can you feel any pulses in your body, for instance, at the temples or the wrists? Breathe in an easy, comfortable rhythm. When you feel finished, you can sit up relaxed and refreshed.

Body temperature is another seemingly involuntary process that can be controlled by the mind. In order to test their meditative abilities, Yogis and Buddhist monks melt the snow around them by meditating on body warming. The following exercise in handwarming offers you a straightforward place to start. We have taught this for years to children and adults. Over time many people have found these skills to be very useful. One child used handwarming before she began to work with clay. Her art teacher said that her clay was always the warmest and softest, thereby making it easy to work.

MEDITATION 2: HANDWARMING

Sit cross-legged on the floor or in a comfortable chair. Before you begin, measure the temperature of your palm by touching it to your upper arm. Notice how warm or cool your hand feels in relation to your arm.

Place your hands together, palm to palm, fingers touching. Close your eyes. Feel the warmth between your palms. Imagine that the warmth grows. Some people like to focus on the feeling of warmth in their hands. Others have imagined placing their hands near a warm fire in the fireplace or have thought of a very hot day with the sun beating down on their hands. Search for an image of warmth that appeals to you. Spend several minutes allowing the warmth to develop. Then test your palm against your arm again. Note any change in temperature. Return to the starting position with palms touching and meditate further. When you are finished, test your hand's temperature again. People are often pleasantly surprised to note a marked warmth in their palms.

If you are a more advanced student, hold your hands, palms facing each other, several inches apart. Feel the heat emanating between the palms. Perform the exercise as described, testing the change in temperature by touching your palm to your upper arm.

MEDITATION 3:
COOL THE FOREHEAD, WARM THE HANDS

Advanced meditators like the challenge of doing two things at once. Once you can perform handwarming at will, try doing several things simultaneously. While warming your hands, direct your attention to your forehead and encourage it to be cool. Some people imagine a cool breeze blowing across their forehead. Others like to invite the mind to find a way to cool the forehead. Experiment with your own ways.

MEDITATION 4: TO EASE PAIN

Healing is an art that has been practiced throughout the centuries. Many qualities of healing with the mind are little understood. Western medicine now admits that the mind can be a great adjunct to healing, sometimes in simple ways. This exercise uses the warmth you create in the handwarming meditation for self-healing. It is best performed after you have successfully warmed your hands.

Do you have an ache or pain right now? Where? For example, is it in your neck or shoulders, your head, or perhaps a sore joint? Turn your attention back to the uncomfortable area. Take

Meditation 4: To Ease Pain, continued

your warmed hands and touch them lightly to your shoulders (or any other sore area). Allow the warmth from your hands to penetrate into the area. Spasms in muscles may let go a bit. Allow the energy to flow freely. The warmth is soothing. Imagine that it spreads throughout the area to be treated.

Do you feel like a slave to temperature? If it is too cold or too warm, do you suffer? Through meditation you can learn to transcend temperature to feel comfortable always.

The experience of temperature is relative. People who live in the north go through months and months of sub-zero temperatures. In Vermont, after a stint of zero-degree weather many natives feel that when the thermometer climbs to zero degrees, it is warm, and they take off their jackets! The opposite is true concerning changes in heat intensity for people who live in the tropics. The personal experience of temperature can vary. On a very hot day, you might have stepped in front of a cool fan and suddenly felt cold. Or perhaps in the middle of winter you wore one sweater too many and felt hot even though you were outdoors in cold air. These subjective perceptions are natural and can be used in meditation to help you transcend physical limitations.

MEDITATION 5: BEYOND TEMPERATURE

Sit comfortably and close your eyes. Experiment briefly with handwarming. Then work with cooling your forehead. Next clear your mind of all concern for temperature by sitting calmly, mind stilled, body at ease. Stay focused as best you can in "no word, no thought, no feel" meditation for several minutes. You are now beyond temperature. We will do more on this in the next chapter.

12
EMPTY THE MIND'S CUP

It is mind that deludes Mind,
For there is no other mind.
O Mind, do not let yourself
Be misled by mind.

—Old Japanese poem cited by
Shunryu Suzuki in *Zen Mind, Beginner's Mind*

One of the great traditions in meditation is clearing the mind. This skill has many indirect, positive effects. Normally, the mind jumps from one set of associations to another. The Buddhists had a name for this common condition: monkey mind. Clear thinking is lost in a sea of many associated thoughts rushing around. Once you learn how to empty your mind, you will be able to think more clearly. With the mind-chatter from the minor concerns of daily life cleared away, you become less scattered, more single-minded and self-directed. Solutions to problems are easier to recognize without extraneous thoughts to distract you. You can respond to situations in a more mature manner.

The untrained person experiences thoughts as occurring automatically, beyond control. Psychology and meditation teach that the contents of your mind can be influenced, just as readily as a sculptor can shape a piece of raw wood into an object of beauty. The interaction of the artist's inner vision with the qualities and capacities of the wood makes this possible. Attention and concentration, applied meditatively, are your tools for refining control of your unconscious mind.

MEDITATION 1: TO FOCUS THE MIND

Sit comfortably in a place where you will be left undisturbed for the time you devote to this meditation. Find a comfortable position. The exact placement of hands and feet is not important, within natural commonsense boundaries. Some people like to sit cross-legged. Others prefer to sit with legs together and pulled in, knees bent, feet flat. Either way is workable as long as the position is comfortable to you. Close your eyes. Focus all your attention on one color, your favorite color, or perhaps white or black. If any thoughts or feelings intrude, try to return your attention to the color you have chosen. At first, concentrate on the color for a brief time only. When you feel ready, open your eyes.

Practice this meditation several times a day at several different sittings. Once you can keep your mind focused for thirty seconds, increase the meditation time to one minute, then two minutes, then up to as long as you like. Some people like to meditate twice a day, for fifteen minutes morning and evening. Find your own rhythms.

MEDITATION 2: BEYOND THOUGHT

In this exercise, you will work with your thoughts to reduce the mental chatter, until it stops. Sit or lie down comfortably. Close your eyes as you did in Meditation 1. If a thought pops into your consciousness, notice it, think about it for a moment if you must, then let it go. Return to your focused attention: poised, observant. When the next thought comes along, do what you did before: notice the thought, think about it briefly if you must, but disengage from it and return to your concentration as soon as you can. Your task is to stay focused. You can think of your mind as a vast river and your thoughts as small leaves or branches floating along. With time and practice, you will be able to watch from the banks of the river and allow the leaves and branches of your thoughts to simply float past, with little notice except to observe that they do move past. Eventually the stream of consciousness clears, and no new thoughts occur. Remain in meditation with a still mind until you feel ready to stop.

MEDITATION 3: TO CLEAR THE MIND

Once you have succeeded at focusing your attention on one thing for several minutes and following your mind to stillness, you are ready to sustain clearing the mind. Let your mind empty of all thought. This means think of nothing, a vast empty space or complete darkness. Begin with thirty seconds and increase as you did when focusing the mind. Regular practice, daily if possible for a few minutes at a time, is all that is required. In time you will find this meditative state quite natural.

MEDITATION 4: TO STILL THE MIND

A lake is an apt metaphor for the mind. Ripples of waves in the water can be like thoughts. Close your eyes. Visualize a beautiful lake. Picture the water as crystal clear and pure. A breeze plays across the surface of the water, causing ripples. These ripples spread outward along the water. Notice this carefully. Then gradually the wind subsides. Watch the ripples dissipate until the lake is calm, clear, and still. It reflects the surroundings. You can see all the way through to the sandy bottom. Enjoy this quiet until you feel ready to open your eyes.

For some people direct meditation is not the best way. If you have found the previous exercises difficult to do, or if you would like to try something different, the following meditation is less active and direct. It will help you still your mind indirectly.

Earlier we wrote about rhythms: rhythms of vital energy, of circulation, and of breathing that are appropriate in various circumstances; cycles that are part of us in ways we hardly know. We all have rhythms of the body and of mental functioning. At certain times of day, or perhaps during the week, or even over the months and seasons, we are spontaneously more physically or mentally active. Some people do their best creating late at night. Others get up early to do creative work. Some people want to get out and do things in the summer, while others prefer the winter. These natural tendencies can be harnessed for meditation. The meditation that follows uses the Taoist strategy of letting be and allowing.

MEDITATION 5: TO OVERCOME RESISTANCE WITH AN INDIRECT APPROACH

Notice a time when you have no immediate responsibilities or obligations, coupled with less spontaneous mental activity. You can utilize that moment of potential readiness and catch yourself when you already have a quiet mind. Spend a few minutes permitting your mind to be empty and explore how expansive that emptiness can be. You do not present what this emptiness is like to yourself exactly, but inner willingness must bond together with natural, spontaneous impulse as one. This state of mind may happen sitting, standing, waiting in line for a long time, or quietly at home. The important thing is to permit the experience to take place if the circumstances are appropriate, and enjoy! After you have allowed your naturally occurring emptiness, even if only for a brief time, you may find that you can deliberately access this emptiness at other times as well. Go back and try some of the other meditations in this chapter again.

Zen Master Seung Sahn has brought Korean Zen to
America and Europe. He is an inspiration to all as a
man of action with a calm, meditative center.
Photo by Lynn Lickteig. Reproduced by permission.

PART FOUR
Mind in Action

If this snail
Sets out for
The top of Fuji
Surely he will
Get there

—Tesshu, Japanese swordsman

Using the principles of mind in action, we may utilize Eastern meditation as a stepping-stone from which to make changes in our everyday life. The following chapters put the mind in action with specific practical applications for your meditative skills. Please feel free to experiment with many contexts. The possibilities are infinite!

13
CALMNESS

The joy of the winds
The dance of the sea
Conscious and unconscious tranquillity.

—Alex Simpkins

editation is known to promote a deep sense of inner calm. Many of the exercises you have performed so far can lead to a calm feeling, which, as a by-product, can help you to cope with stress. The meditations that follow are designed specifically to help you be calmer in your life. Practice them regularly.

STEPS TO CALMNESS

You can present an idea to your unconscious mind, then wait for it to take place. In this meditation, sit or lie down and experiment with using visual imagery to relax.

Imagine that you are climbing down a flight of stairs. You may wish to picture a specific flight of stairs that you use frequently. With each step down, imagine that you become more and more relaxed. When you reach the bottom, you will be completely relaxed. Meditate on the relaxation; experience it all over. What is it like? Now can you imagine calmness sweeping over you and covering you like a comfortable blanket? Let your breathing settle to a calmer, gentler rhythm. You do not have to think of anything in particular, simply wait, to permit a calm feeling to happen. When you feel ready to finish, count backward, suggesting that with each number you will become more and more alert, until you reach one. Then you can be fully alert, yet retain your calm comfortable feeling.

RELAXING MEMORY

All people have had times in their lives when they have felt at ease and calm. Even those who are chronically tense can recall isolated moments when they felt very relaxed. It is possible to draw upon these inner resources for calmness in meditation. The following exercise will help you to find a calmness through memory.

Close your eyes. Let your mind think back to some time or place when you felt very relaxed and at ease. Choose one particular experience. Recall the details. Did it have a distinctive smell, such as the aroma of pine trees in a forest, salt air at the ocean, leather and books in a beloved library? Notice other details. Was there a gentle breeze, warm sun, or even brisk cold? Look around and imagine that you are right there. As you move around or sit in this place and time, observe what you feel. Your muscles will tend to relax. Allow this to occur in its own way. When you are finished, return to the present time and place, relaxed and refreshed. You may allow the experience to linger.

UNCONSCIOUS CALM

When working with your unconscious mind, you can approach relaxation in another way. We use our conscious mind when we tell ourselves to relax, by directing ourselves to tighten muscles and relax them, or by consciously thinking of a relaxing place. Unconscious mind responds differently, often more subtly and indirectly. Unconscious relaxation begins with the genuine wish and intention to relax. You cannot deliberately bring this about.

Sit comfortably and invite yourself to relax. Wonder about how your body will go about it. Will your arms relax first or your legs? Will you feel a comfortable warmth or coolness? Will your mind evoke specific imagery that relaxes you? Wait for your response with open curiosity. The unconscious can surprise you with unexpected, creative responses. You don't know just what form the relaxation will take, but trust that when you are ready, you will become very relaxed.

IMAGINARY STONE SKIPPING

Perform this exercise with your eyes closed. During this visualization, your eyes will relax, along with your mind.

Have you ever skipped stones over the water? To do so you must find a very flat stone and throw it sideways, so that it just touches the water and bounces off, over and over. With practice you may be able to skip the stone seven, eight, or more times. Even if you haven't actually done it yourself, you can probably imagine it. Visualize a calm body of water, such as a lake. Take a few moments to look around you. Do large trees surround the lake? Is there a sandy beach? Can you smell the clean air? Feel a gentle breeze? Imagine that you or someone else steps up to the shore to skip stones. Picture the stone as it skips out along the surface of the water. Imagine that it skips a number of times. Picture it as vividly as you can.

14

ENHANCE THE QUALITY
OF YOUR LIFE

Unified in spirit, what cannot be accomplished?

—Tesshu, Japanese swordsman

E ach of us has daily tasks to perform in our day-to-day lives. Zen teaches that when approached meditatively, every activity, from the moment of arising in the morning to the moment of entering sleep, can take on a special, sensitive quality for inner work. Taoism teaches that when you become one with your activity, permitting your natural responses, you become wiser and gain an infinite reservoir of positive potential for contemplation and learning.

We must cultivate detachment from trivial things in life in order to free ourselves for meditation. To do this, we cannot make too much fuss over whether we are detached or not, since this too, para-doxically, becomes a source of bias or attachment—or "clinging," as the Buddhists refer to it. This moment-to-moment existence is your Reality. Every moment is an opportunity to transcend, while fully experiencing and committing yourself to the circumstances in which you find yourself. When you fully attend to what you do, things lose their trivial quality and you may experience circumstances differently. What creates an experience is not what you do but how you do it, how you relate to it.

JUST WASHING

In this meditation, you can bring your meditative presence to an activity of your choice. Choose something simple that you usually rush through without paying too much attention, because you think of it as a chore. One possibility is washing the dishes or perhaps washing the car. Any activity of this kind can become an opportunity to contemplate.

Before you begin, close your eyes. Clear your mind of thoughts, then sense your body. If you are standing by the sink or beside your car, notice all the details of your experience. Are your arms tense or relaxed in preparation? How do you feel as you are about to engage in washing? Now begin the activity. Feel the sudsy water as you wash. Smell the soap. Watch the dirt as it slides off the surface. Watch the patterns. Listen to the sounds. Keep centered in your experience. When you have finished, close your eyes once more and clear your mind again. Then open your eyes. How do you feel now?

You can try this with many kinds of tasks that are part of your day, but do so one at a time at first. As you advance, practice with your regular daily activity, concentrating on each action of a sequence as you do it. If your mind spontaneously wanders by inattention or otherwise resists, do not worry about it. Accept it, include it as in the clearing mind exercises, and continue to practice. Relax enough to release unnecessary tensions, but not so much as to be unaware or inefficient. You can extend this general attitude into almost any realm of action. The following exercises may help you with this.

IMPROVE YOUR ENVIRONMENT

We busily go about our everyday lives and often do not notice the details of our immediate environment. This meditation can help you to be in a deeper and more sensitive contact with the things around you. When you do this exercise, you will understand how meditation and action are not separate: they are one.

Begin this meditation sitting in your house. Close your eyes and visualize the environment directly outside your home. Do you see other houses, apartments, streets, trees, sidewalks, flowers, trash cans, signs, people? Try to picture everything vividly. Then notice the sounds. Do you hear voices, cars, music, birds? Focus on smells. Is there the smell of automobile exhaust, grass, trees, the aroma from a nearby restaurant, garbage? Do not just categorize; instead experience what is there. Meditate for several minutes on all of these sensations. From the Zen perspective, you could stay focused without using a label or conceptualization to describe the sensations. When you are finished, go outside and survey the area you visualized. Did you remember accurately? What did you leave out? Take a few moments to perceive carefully.

Often when people become more sensitive, they notice things they had not noticed before. You may find that you now perceive some things in your environment that you like and some that you do not like, things that you may have ignored before. If so, ask yourself: Is this something that I can

Improve Your Environment, continued

change? Would I like to change it? If trash is strewn around, you can clean it up in a few hours with a trash bag and rubber gloves. If your fence needs painting, perhaps it is time to devote some free time to this project. Many situations can be improved by making one small change. Experiment, and then notice your response.

15
CONTROL HABITS

Mind power is an actual living force.
—William Walker Atkinson, *Mind Power*

f you have a problem with habit control, meditation offers you a way to resolve it. In meditation to control habits, you must address a task. For example, a client who particularly liked ice cream came to us for help with dieting. After some work with us, she was given a meditative task: to go to a gourmet ice cream parlor with a group of friends, but not to eat. She was delighted to discover that she could enjoy watching her friends have a good time eating but not indulge her own appetite for ice cream. She meditated on the experience while observing and interacting. To her surprise, she was not tortured. Instead, she learned a great deal about impulse and inhibition, companionship and conduct, discipline and determination. Afterward she found it easier to eat more moderately. She continued to enjoy the company of her friends.

Habits can be altered deliberately by a form of Yoga meditation. The method is different from our usual rational, problem-solving approach. Instead, it involves actually altering the focus of attention so that the problem seems to fade away. According to many of the Eastern philosophies described in this book, perceptions are relative and ever-changing, not fixed and set. In the two exercises that follow, you apply your mental skills to alter problematical habits. You can apply the same method to specific habits you wish to change.

This exercise works with your sense of taste. Most people accept their likes and dislikes in food as givens, unless it becomes a problem to them. Taoists know that when we become attuned to deeper levels of understanding, everyday things take on a different significance for us. Meditating on sensory preferences can be an interesting arena for experimentation with this Taoist concept.

A CHANGE OF TASTE

Think about a food that you dislike. Pick a food you mildly dislike for your first experiment. When you have mastered this exercise, challenge yourself with a food you dislike even more. Focus your mind on this one food. Visualize how it looks. Try to look without concern for whether you like it or not. Notice its texture and color. Next imagine the aroma from the food. Then imagine the taste. Analyze the taste: notice whether it is salty, sweet, sour, or bitter. After you have focused deeply upon these sensory experiences, prepare this food to eat. Notice everything about it that you did in meditation. Take a small taste of the food. Do not swallow it immediately, but allow yourself to notice all the qualities: temperature, flavor, whether it tastes bitter, sweet, sour, or salty. Suspend judgment for now and simply experience it deeply. Repeat this experiment at several different times.

A CHANGE OF HABIT

Pick a habit that you wish you could stop doing. Through this exercise, you will deliberately begin to give up the habit. Begin by closing your eyes and imagining a situation where you usually do this habit. Here are two examples, but feel free to substitute a habit that bothers you. If you are trying to cut down on spending money for clothes or food, imagine that you are in your favorite clothing or food store, admiring all the stylish clothes or gourmet food, but that after enjoying looking, you leave without buying and feel fine with this. Focus vividly on this imaginary scenario and make it as real as possible for yourself. Think of possible satisfactions you could gain from looking, such as coming up with a new way to combine the clothes you already have or a different way to use one of your usual foods. After you have practiced this imaginary meditation several times over a span of days or weeks, actually go to the clothing or food store you imagined and do exactly as you visualized. Be certain to leave without buying anything. Later, notice how you felt. Repeat the exercise several times. Does the experience change for you? How do you experience your pattern over time?

A MANAGEABLE CHANGE

If you find changing your habits particularly difficult, try breaking the action down into smaller steps and then rehearsing each step. First, imagine that you go to the vicinity of the store, then leave. Next imagine that you walk up to the door, then turn around and leave. Break the problem behavior down into manageable steps. Backtrack if you need to in order to get it exactly correct. Then practice the real thing, step by step. First, drive or walk to the store, but do not go in. Next, walk into the store, stay only a moment, then leave. In manageable chunks, go through to the point of completion, of leaving without buying. The bothersome habit now becomes an opportunity to learn something useful instead of being a pesky nuisance.

16
PROBLEM SOLVING

You should rather be grateful for the weeds you have in your mind, because eventually they will enrich your practice.

—Shunryu Suzuki, *Zen Mind, Beginner's Mind*

T he regular practice of meditation leads to an alteration of perspective. You can use the meditative perspective, which is different from conventional thinking, to solve problems in everyday life.

YIN AND YANG

Extend perception beyond its usual boundaries to solve problems. The yin-yang, in its expression as opposites, can be used to foster new ideas and perspectives.

According to Isaac Newton, for every force there is an equal and opposite counterforce. Thus, an "opposite" is part of any extension of force, so to speak. Sometimes, by imaginatively considering the opposite, we can free our perception: it may be that the contrast assists in clarifying boundaries. Then you may find the balance point.

REVERSING PERSPECTIVE

Pick a problem that bothers you. Close your eyes and clear your mind. If you have difficulty, refer back to chapter 12 on clearing the mind. Practice regularly. Once you can produce a clear, calm mind, you will be ready to apply that mind. Now focus on the problem that is bothering you. Using your meditation skills, consider the problem from another perspective. Imagine its opposite. For example, if you are annoyed with someone, can you imagine the situation from that person's point of view? What would it be like to have someone else annoyed with you, as you feel toward the other person? Can you imagine how the other person might be experiencing you and thus gain empathy? After you have spent some time contemplating, allow yourself to relax. Gradually new patterns of meaning will emerge.

Now consider what it would be like if you did not have this problem. What is your life like without it? How are you different?

For a variation, imagine if you had the opposite problem. For example, if overeating is your difficulty, what would it be like to lose too much weight? Can you use your creativity to alter your situation? Many things have a use and meaning that we might never imagine from our usual perspective.

Use these examples as analogies to think of other opposites, other solutions.

Drawing from Christmas Humphreys' approach (1971), we may adapt the Zen frame of reference for practical problem solving. To begin, put everything into perspective. Buddhism holds that things are not what they seem. Nothing actually exists, we are not real, nor is the everyday world real. In a philosophical sense, all that we experience is illusion, transitory, ever-changing. The "I"—that is, ourselves—and the "it"—the situation—are concepts, products of our own mind, subject to distortion, bias, or even delusion. These illusions may obstruct spontaneous, correct responses. Beginning with this frame of reference, approach the problem recognizing that it is not a permanent condition, even if it feels that way to you at the moment. This moment is also in flux and does not necessarily reflect what the future must be. We as human beings must face each situation as best we can, accepting that many forces are always at play. No situation is isolated or fixed for all time. Buddhism teaches that there is a larger Universal Oneness, a tapestry of many threads interwoven together, within which everything and everyone is all right and in an orderly relationship. We all partake of this, and so it is important to reassure yourself that ultimately everything will work out for the best. There is an inner logic within the way of things. This mind-set helps you to prepare yourself properly to make some change.

MEDITATIVE DETACHMENT TO SOLVE PROBLEMS

Pick a problem, a small one to start with, that you need to address. Now begin to work on your response to the problem. Instead of indulging in strong emotional reactions, try to face the situation with steadiness, neither approving nor disapproving; simply focus directly on the problem with a clear mind. Try to set aside personal feelings of pride or embarrassment, anger or distress, to view matters as they are in a larger context. Using the clarity of meditation, notice all the details of the situation as it is, without judgment.

Finally, you are ready to take action. In realizing that there is no division between subject and object, between you and your situation, you can face it and respond to it fully and appropriately. If you respond fully, from a meditative state of

> **Meditative Detachment to Solve Problems, continued**
>
> mind, a "right response" will emerge that is ethical, at one with the situation, and also in tune with the lawfulness of the higher reality.

WHAT IS THE TRUE NATURE OF THE PROBLEM?

Many times people mistake what the true nature of their problem really is. For example, a person who was afraid to fly made no progress when she tried to address this particular fear. Through a hypnotic trance and working with renowned hypnotherapist Milton Erickson, she discovered that she actually was afraid of enclosed spaces. When she was confined in the cabin of a plane in flight, she felt fearful and assumed that fear of flying was the cause. Dr. Erickson helped her to look for the real problem, and change it using hypnotic trance. Her fear vanished once she was comfortable in the enclosed space of the cabin. She even enjoyed flying! Many problems are like this. The cause of the problem is hidden, but it connects and restrains like the links in a chain to an anchor in the depths far below.

17
CULTIVATE LEARNING

*Man's power to change himself, that is, to learn, is per-
haps the most impressive thing about him.*

—E. L. Thorndike, *Human Learning*

tudents will find meditation an invaluable tool to help with
studies. Many of the exercises presented earlier in the
book, such as clearing your mind, relaxing your body, and
focusing your attention, can be used to enhance learning. Review the
chapters that cover these topics.

People can concentrate most successfully when their mind is
clear and ready. Often students begin their homework after a long,
hard day at school. They will be far more productive if they relax their
mind first.

PRELIMINARY WARM-UPS TO STUDY

Lie down. Close your eyes and relax your body as much as possible. Allow your breathing to quiet into a rhythm that feels easy and natural. Rest comfortably for a few minutes. Next, imagine a very pleasant place where you feel calm and at ease. Perhaps it is a place in nature, a museum, or at home with your favorite music. Recall a time when you were there, perhaps during a vacation, after exams, when you did not feel pressured. Imagine vividly that you are there now. Try to bring the experience clearly into the foreground. Let all your current concerns temporarily shift into the background. Enjoy that feeling for a few moments. Then return to the here and now and open your eyes. You may stretch or move a little to reorient yourself to the present.

After you feel relaxed, you may want to revitalize your energy. Review the internal energy exercises from chapter 10 and perform them to renew your vitality. Try to be sensitive to what you need. Are your muscles tight? Then attempt to let go of excess tightness. Are you nervous about a test or an assignment? If so, you may find it helpful to reflect meditatively, using some of the problem-solving techniques from chapter 16.

WANDERING ATTENTION

The following exercises can help to improve control over wandering attention during studies.

Now that you have enjoyed some relaxed moments, turn to your studies for a short but intense period, perhaps thirty minutes. Before you become fatigued, shift back to your imaginary relaxed place for a five- or ten-minute break. Then return to your studies for a set period followed by another five- or ten-minute meditative break. Shift regularly back and forth in this way throughout your study period. If you notice that your attention fades sooner during a study period, take an extra relaxation break. Conversely, if you can concentrate longer, do so. Not only will you be able to learn better, but you will find that you have greater endurance to study longer. Chart your rhythms of rest and of concentration so that you can anticipate them correctly.

ATTENTION TO STUDIES

The exercise that follows improves the quality of your attention to studies.

Sit comfortably or lie down. Close your eyes. Focus your mind on the subject you are trying to study. Think carefully about some aspect of it. Imagine a searchlight in your mind that shines light on the material, scanning. Mentally review the information under the light. Concentrate the light like a spotlight on any necessary specific areas. Then turn the light off. Be comfortable. Next turn the searchlight on again. Focus all your attention on the material. Do you notice more? Picture it vividly. Turn on the "mind's light" as often as needed.

MEDITATIVE REVIEW

To study for a test or to master material, you can use meditative skills in visualization and relaxation to help you make the material truly yours.

There comes a point toward the end of your study session when you have, in a sense, inputted the material into your mental computer. At this point, lie on the floor or sit in a comfortable chair where you can lean back. Mentally lay out the material you have studied. You may want to do it visually, as picturing the pages in the book you studied, or you might prefer a more general schematic or outline. Pay attention to the concepts and how they connect. Review lists, ideas: whatever is relevant. Calmly meditate on the material as it sorts and settles. When you are finished, you will find that after your study session, you can focus on the material with more clarity and understanding.

ONE WITH YOUR SUBJECT

Students often fight against themselves when trying to learn. The Taoists believe that when you become one with something, you will know it fully and naturally, without effort. This belief can be used for learning.

Consider a subject that you are studying, for example, chemistry. Aside from your regular work on memorization, labs, and calculations, consider how chemistry surrounds you. Think of the common, everyday examples of chemistry in your life, such as boiling water for tea. Allow yourself to become interested and curious about chemistry. When you are in the lab, occasionally set aside the experiment for a moment to experience what you are doing fully. Be present in the moment, in a meditative sense, and observe without analysis or judgment. Let the situation be and try not to interfere with it. Relax your body as much as possible and breathe naturally. Then the experiment can speak to you, unobstructed. As you learn to do this well, become the experience as fully as you can.

As a second exercise, apply this to another subject. History students could think of yesterday's events as mini-history. Let yourself think about each subject in a playful, imaginative way. Get involved. Go to a museum or historical site that is connected to the subject. Imagine yourself back in that time period, immersed in the events. Contemplate the tie-ins. You will undoubtedly have your own thoughts and insights about them.

Another way to stimulate this experience is to browse through books on the subject at a bookstore or watch a historical video. Find a fun novel set in that time period. Even if the material is on a simple level, it serves to get you involved,

One with Your Subject, continued

searching beyond the details to be at one with the subject's personal meaning for you. Then you will be like the sages of old who sought not just knowledge but wisdom.

18

IMPROVE YOUR SPORTS PERFORMANCE

---

*The physical training and the mastery of technique are
no doubt essential, but he who lacks psychic training is
sure to be defeated. While being trained in the art, the
pupil is to be active and dynamic in every way. But in
actual combat, his mind must be calm and not at all
disturbed.*

—Masahiro Adachi, teacher of swordsmanship

thletes often use meditation to improve their performance.
Martial artists have long been known for their mental training, which helps them overcome barriers to do impossible
feats, such as breaking wood and concrete blocks. These astounding
abilities begin within the mind. Athletes of all spo.ts can benefit from
meditation's "mind first." The exercises that follow are specifically
designed for athletes in any sport. You also can adapt any of the meditations presented earlier in the book to improve sports performance.

MUSCLE CONTROL

Many sports require control of body movements beyond the normal
needs of everyday life. At times we all move easily without thought.
Moving steadily on a gymnastics balance beam only a few inches
wide, or throwing a baseball or football, or performing a side kick in
martial arts with strength and accuracy to break multiple boards

requires exacting and complex combinations of muscle contractions timed with relaxation. Great athletes know that being able to be loose or tight when needed allows for flexible and quick motions that are also powerful. Review the meditations on general body relaxation in chapter 8 before trying this exercise.

RELAXING THE MUSCLES

Lie on the floor, on your back. Relax your body and close your eyes. Scan through your muscles with your awareness. If you notice any tight muscles, try to relax them. Raise your right arm so that it points straight up. Make a fist and tighten the muscles of your hand and arm. As you tighten your raised arm, keep the rest of your body relaxed. There is a natural tendency to tighten the other arm or the shoulders and neck. Resist this impulse and keep relaxed. Hold your right arm tense for approximately thirty seconds, then let it down and relax. Repeat this exercise with the other arm and then each leg, one at a time. The ability to concentrate on different muscle groups will prove valuable for many sports.

FOCUS IN SPORTS

Direct your attention selectively to your sports activity. We will use jogging as an example, but you can apply this exercise to anything that involves movement. When you go for a jog (swim, golf game, etc.), notice how your feet hit the ground as you run. What do you feel in your legs? Are your muscles tight? What about your arms? Observe how they swing as you run. Can you permit them to find a natural rhythm? Are your shoulders relaxed? Is your stride flowing and unified with the rest of your body? If you can, permit your body to relax as much as possible as you run, letting go of unnecessary tension. Allow yourself to move at your natural pace. Notice your breathing. Is it smooth and regular, or forced and uneven? Can you allow it to find the appropriate rhythm for the time? Pay attention to the details of your sensory experience, instead of exerting any control. In active moments, when you are fully focused on action and are one with your intent to run, do you really experience any difficulty?

An alternative meditation method is to focus on a single thought, perhaps an image, a point in space, your breathing, or even a blank mind while you run. Allow your body to move automatically, flowing naturally. For some people, restricting their awareness to a small focus is best, while others find it better to expand their thoughts to a larger focus. Either method is acceptable, depending on the needs of the individual.

Ancient Japanese swordsmen understood that there comes a point when the practitioner must set aside technique.

Their mind works in the busiest possible way on how best to make use of all the tactics they have learned. They have no idea whatever of Heavenly Reason and its functioning under varying conditions. The great mistake in swordsmanship is to anticipate the outcome of the engagement; you ought not to be thinking of whether it ends in victory or defeat. Just let Nature take its course, and your sword will strike at the right moment. (Ichiun quoted in D. T. Suzuki 1959, 174)

As a trained athlete, you can develop an inner trust that your skills will be expressed when needed. Use meditation to clear your mind and move naturally, without thought, with your sport.

Readiness of mind is an important aspect of performance, profoundly affecting actions. Mary Lou Retton, Olympic gymnast, "set" herself for all movement effort. She paused first, envisioned her entire routine, then cleared her mind to be ready. A certain world-class martial arts champion always set his mind before a tournament bout by performing a short ritual of stretches followed by a yell. Many athletes know that the difference between victory and defeat is often a matter of who had the mental edge.

NO MIND IN SPORT

Begin to train your mind before each practice session. Do the following meditation before the actual competition. Ensure that you have trained hard and well—overtrain, in fact, so that you do not need to think about any movements. They will arise spontaneously as needed. If you have trained properly, you can trust in yourself.

Center yourself in the present. Do not move beyond this moment. Stay with the now. When you are ready to perform, clear your mind. Perform as if for the first time, with no past history of either success or failure. For example, if you are a golfer, play each hole as if it were the first. Let the game take care of itself. Do your best at the time, with nothing to hold you back. As you perform your sport, fill your mind only with your action in the moment, nothing else.

CONCLUSION

Meditation
Better than anything
Can restore us
To inner wellsprings
Helps us shed all cares for now
Cools and soothes the soul
Clears the mind
Makes us whole.

—Alex Simpkins

Meditation helps us to dispel illusions and experience life more fully. When we become truly centered in our experience, in the meditative sense, we are well-oriented and comfortable with ourselves and our lives. Our life becomes more productive and compassionate.

Meditation may use many levels of the mind. The art of meditation can lead to an actualization of the whole person, a unification of the conscious and the unconscious mind. All your faculties—your attention and concentration, visualization and imagination, senses, body and mind—become one. At these moments, an integration takes place, and you are fully yourself, expressive in the meditative moment. You experience what has been called higher consciousness, self-actualization, true insight.

The art of meditation revolves around permitting your unconscious and conscious mind to blend and compound, so that they enrich each other. Meditation is an opportunity to reintegrate and find your true nature through the use of your many abilities. Thinking things through and problem solving may occur naturally when your mind is clear and your whole nature is sensitively attuned in focused meditation. Problems also may seem easier to resolve. Apply meditation to your life, and you will overcome barriers and evolve beyond them.

JUST MEDITATE

As you explored the way of meditation, you have experimented with many different approaches. Now, with nothing in mind, simply walk the path, and may you be in meditation always.

BIBLIOGRAPHY

Alexander, C. N., et al., "Transcendental Meditation, Mindfulness, and Longevity," *Journal of Personality and Social Psychology* 57, no. 6 (1989): 950–64.

Atkinson, W. W. *Mind Power*. Chicago: Yogi Publication Society, 1912.

Bates, W. H., and Macfadden, B. *Strengthening the Eyes*. New York: Physical Culture Publishing Co., 1918.

Beck, L. A. *The Story of Oriental Philosophy*. New York: New Home Library, 1928.

Bhikshu. *Karma Yoga*. Chicago: Yogi Publication Society, 1928.

Blyth, R. H. *Zen and Zen Classics*, vols. 1, 2. Tokyo: Hokuseido Press, 1960.

Campbell, J. *The Masks of God: Oriental Philosophy*. New York: Viking Press, 1962.

Chan, Wing-Tsit. *A Source Book in Chinese Philosophy*. Princeton, NJ: Princeton University Press, 1963.

Duyvendak, J. J. L. *Tao te Ching, The Book of the Way and Its Virtue*. Boston: Charles E. Tuttle Co., Inc., 1992.

Henricks, R. G., trans. *Lao-Tzu Te-Tao Ching*. New York: Ballantine Books, 1989.

Humphreys, C. *A Western Approach to Zen*. Wheaton, IL: The Theosophical Publishing House, 1971.

Husserl, E. *The Idea of Phenomenology*. The Hague: Martinus Nijhoff, 1964.

James, W. *The Principles of Psychology*. New York: Henry Holt & Company, 1896.

Jaspers, K. *Socrates Buddha Confucius Jesus*. New York: Harvest HBJ Book, 1962.

Kaptchuk, T. J. *The Web That Has No Weaver*. New York: Congdon & Weed, 1983.

Keene, B. *Sensing, Letting Yourself Live*. New York: Harper & Row, 1979.

Legge, J. *The Texts of Taoism*, vols. 1, 2. New York: Dover, 1962.

Liu, D. *T'ai Chi Ch'uan and Meditation*. New York: Schocken Books, 1986.

Merton, T. *Mystics and Zen Masters*. New York: Noonday Press, 1967.

———. *Zen and the Birds of Appetite*. New York: New Directions Publishing Corp., 1968.

Miura, I., and Sasaki, R. F. *The Zen Koan, Its History and Use in Rinzai Zen*. San Diego: Harvest HBJ Book, 1965.

Norman, D. A. *Memory & Attention*. New York: John Wiley & Sons, 1969.

Pine, R. *The Zen Teaching of Bodhidharma*. San Francisco: North Point Press, 1989.

Ramacharaka. *Advanced Course in Yogi Philosophy and Oriental Occultism*. Chicago: Yoga Publication Society, 1908.

———. *Science of Breath*. Chicago: Yoga Publication Society, 1904.

———. *A Series of Lessons in Raja Yoga*. Chicago: Yoga Publication Society, 1934.

Reps, P. *Zen Flesh, Zen Bones*. Rutland, VT: Charles E. Tuttle Co., Inc., 1980.

Rieber, R. W. *Wilhelm Wundt and the Making of a Scientific Psychology*. New York: Plenum Press, 1980.

Rossi, E., ed. *The Collected Papers of Milton H. Erickson*. New York: Irvington Publishers, 1980.

Samuels, M., and Samuels, N. *Seeing with the Mind's Eye*. New York: Random House, 1975.

Selver, C., and Brooks, C. *Sensory Awareness*. Santa Barbara, CA: Ross Erickson, 1982.

Simpkins, C. A., and Simpkins, A. M. *Principles of Self-Hypnosis, Pathways to the Unconscious*. New York: Irvington, 1991.

Soeng, M. *Thousand Peaks*. Berkeley: Parallax Press, 1987.

Suzuki, D. T. *Zen and Japanese Culture*. Princeton, NJ: Princeton University Press, 1959.

Suzuki, S. *Zen Mind, Beginner's Mind*. New York: Weatherhill, 1979.

Thorndike, E. L. *Human Learning*. Cambridge, MA: M.I.T. Press, 1977.

Watts, A. *The Way of Zen*. New York: Vintage Books, 1957.

Welch, H. *Taoism*. Boston: Beacon Press, 1965.

Yanagi, S. *The Unknown Craftsman, A Japanese Insight into Beauty*. New York: Kodansha International, 1972.

Yang, J-M. *Chi Kung*. Jamaica Plain, MA: YMAA Publication Center, 1985.

Yutang, Lin, ed. *The Wisdom of China and India*. New York: Random House, 1942.